Special Praise for
Becoming a Doctors' Doctor: A Memoir

"In *Becoming a Doctor's Doctor*, noted psychiatrist and educator Michael F. Myers offers a poignant, discerning and hopeful account of the mental health struggles of physicians and of his own career devoted to helping them overcome these challenges. Myers grapples with complex and unsettling topics including suicide, marital breakdown, and mortality with candor and compassion. By sharing of himself and revealing his own vulnerabilities—from growing up with an alcoholic parent to confronting the AIDS epidemic in Vancouver to mourning colleagues lost to COVID-19, he conveys the deep humanity and generosity of spirit that makes him both a gifted clinician and a skilled writer. With this rich and rewarding memoir, Myers assures his place alongside Selzer, Sacks, Verghese, and the rare breed of healer who can work true magic both inside a hospital and on the printed page. Compelling and enlightening." Jacob M. Appel, MD, Assistant Professor Psychiatry. Icahn School of Medicine at Mt Sinai. New York, NY. Bioethicist and Author of Who Says You're Dead?

"The memoir by Michael Myers, "Becoming a Doctors' Doctor," is simply beautiful. His personal story - of 'otherness,' understanding, self-compassion, and courage - will inspire and move all who read this memoir, and it is told with humility and sincerity. My sense is that psychiatrists early in their careers will love this book because it shows so clearly a life of purpose. Psychiatrists in the middle of their careers will appreciate the depth and sophistication of Michael's craft as a therapist and physician. Psychiatrists later in their careers will feel a kinship with Michael - and, still, will find themselves learning as they read his words." Laura Roberts, MD, MA, DLFAPA, FACLP Chair, Katharine Dexter McCormick and Stanley McCormick Memorial Professor, Department of Psychiatry and Behavioral Sciences, Stanford University School of Medicine.

"In an era of everchanging healthcare paradigms, physician wellbeing is paramount. Dr. Myers shares a thoughtful memoir and lessons learnt through personal reflection, resilience and pure perseverance to serve those who serve others. So that we too can heal, Dr. Myers' call to 'heal thine own' is a powerful call to all physicians who enter this profession to serve our patients. Care must start with us." Susan Moffatt-Bruce, MD, PhD, FRCSC. Chief Executive Officer. Royal College of Physicians and Surgeons of Canada.

"In a humbling and humane account of one psychiatrist's journey through life looking after doctors and medical students who develop mental illnesses, this book illustrates what clinical psychiatry is about. Using terrifically moving case histories, Dr Myers illustrates why psychiatry is the best medical specialty and what can be achieved with intellectual curiosity. His humanity, compassion, commitment, kindness and care for his patients makes this a wonderful must-read for clinicians and educators." Dinesh Bhugra, MBBS, PhD, MPhil, MSc, MA.

Emeritus Professor of Mental Health and Cultural Diversity at the Institute of Psychiatry, Psychology and Neuroscience at King's College London. Past President of the Royal College of Psychiatrists and the World Psychiatric Association.

"*Becoming a Doctors' Doctor* reminds us of the importance of témoignage – the French word meaning to bear witness. As psychiatry residents looking to continue the work that Prof Myers started, we must bear witness to the suffering of our colleagues and speak out against structural barriers to physician health. This is not a selfish act – the wellbeing of society depends on our own health. It was Emerson who wrote that success is 'to know that one has breathed easier because you have lived.' The clinical work of Prof Myers has allowed many hundreds, if not thousands, of doctors to breathe easier. His written work, including this book, has a much broader reach. Doctors all over the world can read *Becoming a Doctors' Doctor* and know they are not alone." Malcolm Forbes, MBBS, Clinical Senior Fellow, Department of Psychiatry University of Melbourne, Melbourne, Australia.

"Dr. Michael Myers' memoir is an inspirational story of a physician whose entire career has been devoted to a very neglected and hidden specialty – physician mental health. His skillful writing blends an incredible personal journey of becoming a psychiatrist, a scholar, and an educator, along with a variety of clinical vignettes. Every medical student, resident and physician can learn from this memoir – the clinical acumen and, what's truly poignant, the humanness of a remarkable doctors' doctor." Wei-Yi Song, MD, FRCPC. Clinical Professor, Faculty of

Medicine, University of British Columbia and past president Canadian Psychiatric Association.

"Dr. Michael Myers has spent his professional life devoted to his fellow physicians. He has comforted them when they break down in tears. He has stood by them when they face adversity. He has confronted them when they are thinking about suicide but hiding their plan from their peers. And he has educated them about the perils of overwork. In all instances he has done his job with compassion, grace, caring, and wisdom. In this memoir he shares his experience with all of us who have taken the oath and tried to practice the best medicine we can while recognizing our limits. It is a 'must read'!" Glen O. Gabbard, MD Clinical Professor of Psychiatry, Baylor College of Medicine.

"This book is a gem. Through the eyes of a physician, whose professional and personal life has straddled medicine and psychiatry, we learn so much about the culture of medicine and the minds of doctors. We learn that doctors are not invincible. That they struggle to accept that they too can become patients. We learn also about the joy of medicine - written so eloquently by Michael as he takes us through his personal journey from medical school onwards. A wonderful read and accessible to all." Dr Clare Gerada, MBE FRCP FRCGP FRCPsych, Director, Practitioner Health Programme Hurley Group, London.

"In this compelling read, Dr. Myers traces his evolution as a care giver to care givers who themselves become care receivers. With a steady and deft hand arising from a lifetime of rich clinical experience, he describes his own evolution, doctoring to his colleagues with great compassion and humanity. This is a beautifully written book for all of us, physicians and non-physicians, who wish to peek inside the inner sanctum as a skilled clinician learns from his patients as much as they do from him. Dr. Myers imparts well-earned wisdom, born in courage, that shines a light on our own pathways towards our better selves." John Budin, M.D. is a psychiatrist with bipolar disorder and serves on the Board of Directors of the Depression and Bipolar Support Alliance.

"This memoir reflects an extraordinary openness and humanity, rarely seen in physicians who have learned to conceal their human vulnerability, not only from others but from themselves. Dr Myers' patients are living, breathing human beings, not dry, academic case histories. Their humanity always takes precedence over his clinical or academic skills or competence. Dr Myers provides extraordinary detail in cases treated 40 years ago. It's as if he were currently treating the patient. Hopefully, reading this memoir may encourage more doctors to seek treatment and recognize its benefits." John Tamerin, MD, private practice Greenwich, Connecticut and Clinical Associate Professor at Weill Cornell Medical College in New York City.

"'Becoming a Doctors' Doctor: A Memoir' by Michael F Myers, MD is a sheer masterpiece. Dr Myers's wisdom, compassion, erudition, empathy, knowledge, humility and grace permeates throughout his poignant and powerful narrative. I was utterly gripped and enthralled by the intriguing insights that he shared from decades of treating physicians with mental health difficulties. Reading this memoir has broadened the inner landscapes of my mind and expanded the chambers of my heart. I was so over-whelmed by the beauty of the prose that I was reduced to tears. EVERY psychiatrist must read this book..." Dr Ahmed Hankir MBChB MRCPsych, Academic Clinical Fellow in Psychiatry, Institute of Psychiatry, Psychology and Neuroscience, King's College London, Royal College of Psychiatrists award-winning doctor.

"I love this book! Dr. Myers opens himself up through his per-sonal and professional experiences to reveal the healer that he is. All readers will find comfort in his words, lessons from his medical expertise, and healing from his psychiatric insights. I highly recommend *Becoming a Doctor's Doctor*, especially in these exceptional times, and thank Dr. Myers for leading the way in offering guidance and hope to every one of us." Carla Fine, New York City, author of *No Time to Say Goodbye: Surviving the Suicide of a Loved One.*

"In this personal memoir by Dr Myers, *Becoming a Doctors' Doctor*, we are privileged to read about his life's work and gain an in-timate insight into this great man. The way we view and treat doctors who are ill has changed significantly, and it is largely thanks to the dedication and advocacy of people like Dr Myers that this change has been possible. He tells his profound stories in such a simple, humble way, a way that is deeply moving, inspiring and enriching, and through his lens we see others and ourselves as the beautiful beings we all are. Anne Malatt, MBBS, Ophthalmologist, Alstonville, Australia and author *To Medicine with Love.*

"Dr. Myers is the Paulo Freire of modern medicine. His life story, deeply rooted in courage, compassion and expertise, proves that one person can liberate an entire group of professionals from suffering. Impossible to put down, Dr. Myers' latest and most personal book, will bring smiles and tears to readers." Derek Puddester, MD, FRCPC. Associate Professor Psychiatry University of Ottawa Canada.

"Becoming a Doctors' Doctor: A Memoir" is a moving, deeply personal, account of one psychiatrist's lifelong dedication to understanding and caring for an overlooked and vulnerable population—our physicians. Through Dr Myers' eyes, the reader gains insight into the unique and often heartbreaking struggles of physicians, particularly those with psychiatric illness. By accompanying him along his compelling personal and professional journey, the reader comes to understand what has driven Dr Myers to do such difficult work, and why we all must become advocates for system changes that enable our physicians to embrace their own humanity." Heather Farley, MD, MHCDS, FACEP. Chief Wellness Officer ChristianaCare Newark, DE and Associate Professor of Emergency Medicine Sidney Kimmel Medical College at Thomas Jefferson University, Philadelphia PA.

"Becoming a Doctors' Doctor: A Memoir" is a joy to read. Interweaving his own journey through medicine with gripping stories of his physician patients' experiences, Dr. Myers lays bare the toll our medical system has on physicians but also highlights the joy and humanity of medicine and a pathway to a brighter future. I will certainly be a better caregiver to my physician patients because I read this book." Srijan Sen M.D. Ph.D. Frances and Kenneth Eisenberg Professor of Depression and Neurosciences. Associate Vice President for Research – Health Sciences. University of Michigan.

"An inspirational, insightful and soothing book from a pioneer and mentor in the field of physician help. Dr. Myers shares his lifelong commitment and endeavour in caring for the mental health and wellbeing of physicians and their loved-ones. This is an essential reading to us all, wounded healers who are suffering in silence and in shame, as it celebrates humanness through compassion, empathy, acceptance and, most importantly, hope. Manon Charbonneau, MD, FRCPC, DFCPA. Assistant Clinical Professor, Department of Psychiatry and Addictology. University of Montreal. Bell Let's Talk 2019 Ambassador.

"'Becoming A Doctor's Doctor: A Memoir' is at times, heart rending and revealing, a fascinating mixture of clinical cases, personal reflections and sincerity. What shines through is Dr Myers' care for his colleagues. He leads the reader on a voyage through forty years of medical history and attitudinal changes towards psychiatrically ill physicians, occurring in parallel with major changes in his own life, all addressed with honesty, warmth and insight. This is a book discussing the past, that is about the future. It will be of interest to anyone who cares about the health of physicians." Peter Yellowlees MBBS, MD. Chief Wellness Officer UCD Health. Allan Stoudemire Endowed Professor of Psychiatry, University of California Davis.

"Dr. Myers delights as an engaging storyteller who masterfully weaves stories from his childhood and medical training with patient encounters. We learn of his journey in becoming the "doctors' doctor" as we glimpse into his professional and personal life. His humanity, compassion, and unwavering commitment to physician health is felt on every page and with every word." Dr. F. Gigi Osler BScMed, FRCSC. Assistant Professor, Department of Otolaryngology-Head and Neck Surgery, University of Manitoba. Past President, Canadian Medical Association.

"Prof Michael Myers has written a book which is searing in its honesty about doctors (physicians) as patients and his growth as a doctors' doctor. These are moving stories of doctors' struggle with mental illness which resonated with me as a Psychiatrist starting my journey in this field. Prof Myers packs his learning and expertise honed over a long career into a book joined by a silver thread of compassion and warmth. I hope no doctor feels alone or isolated after reading this book, which above all provides hope." Dr Ananta Dave MBBS, MD, DNB, FRCPsych, MMedEth, Consultant Psychiatrist and Medical Director Lincolnshire Partnership NHS Foundation Trust. Churchill Fellow 2019 wcmt.org.uk. President, British Indian Psychiatrists Association.

"Reading Dr Myers' memoir brought back many instances from my own clinical experiences and my recent years as a medical student affairs director trying to support colleagues and wrestle with social, bureaucratic and academic stigma around emotional distress and mental illness. I know we are making progress but self-stigma amongst health professionals still impedes help seeking. I lost a dedicated colleague to suicide last year and was chagrined to realize that she had attempted to manage her illness largely on her own. It is my hope that this book, replete with poignant honest stories about the privilege and pain that comes from being a doctor, will help guide our colleagues to do better for themselves so that we can be the healers we have worked so hard to become." Pamela Forsythe, MD, FRCPC. Chair Board of Directors and past president Canadian Psychiatric Association Ottawa.

"In this memoir, Dr. Michael Myers reflects on his life's journey as a psychiatrist treating physicians grappling with mental illness. Through a thoughtful choice of personal and professional narratives, Dr. Myers illuminates how the intermingling of one's professional calling and one's humanity shape a remarkable life. Dr. Myers shares intimate personal milestones with candour and self-compassion, while discerningly exposing how physicians are human and also suffer mental illness. The reader, witness to treatment triumphs and tragedies buffered by a physician with boundless wisdom and humanity, comes to truly understand why Dr. Myers is known as the Doctors' Doctor." Jane B. Lemaire MD FRCPC. General Internist, Clinical Professor, Vice Chair Physician Wellness and Vitality, Department of Medicine, Director of Wellness, Office of Professionalism, Equity and Diversity, Wellness Lead, W21C Research and Innovation Center, Cumming School of Medicine, University of Calgary & Physician Lead, Well Doc Alberta.

"Dr Myers leads us through the journey that has made him a skilled clinician, educator and advocate. Outstanding compassion, courage, hope, respect, humility and caring are at the core of all his clinical vignettes. The medical profession should certainly be grateful for his presence as a lighthouse in the dark for so many students, residents, physicians and for those who train to treat them." Renée Roy, MD, FRCP, Forensic Psychiatrist, Institut Philippe-Pinel de Montréal and past president Canadian Psychiatric Association.

"As a doctor in addiction recovery, I've been blessed to develop a professional friendship with Dr. Myers over the last several years. He is a remarkable man and a kind, compassionate and dedicated physician. Yet, in this friendship I never knew the passion behind the portrait of a man, the trauma behind the teaching or the doubt behind the dutiful work. This book beautifully shares the journey of a man seeking out his own calling, forged by the experiences of his youth, early career and with a constant willingness to be changed. I am grateful to know Dr. Myers and continue to be inspired by his work to help other medical professionals." Adam B Hill, MD. Associate Professor of Clinical Pediatrics. Indiana University School of Medicine and author of "Long Walk Out of the Woods."

"This stellar memoir follows the inimitable Dr. Michael Myers from his small-town Ontario home with family secrets to medical school where his first year classmate dies by suicide, through an internship at Los Angeles County Medical Centre, work as an emergency room physician in Detroit, and an internal medicine residency in Los Angeles that leads him to undertake a psychiatry residency and career in Vancouver as the doctors' doctor before transitioning to New York City. Dr. Myers' career journey weaves the personal and the professional right up to the crisis of COVID-19. This book is so compelling that it is the first memoir I have sacrificed sleep for in order to read cover to cover in a single sitting." Susan Abbey, MD, FRCP Psychiatrist-in-Chief, University Health Network. Professor, University of Toronto.

"This beautifully crafted memoir interweaves stories of physicians' lives in which each of us can see a common thread from our own humanness. The work reveals it is exactly those 'dark and frightening feelings' which make us more connected than our isolating mind allows us to believe. Each story enveloped a truth to take away. I now understand Dr. Myers' life-long commitment to reaching out to all physicians who make visible their painful personal struggles. We are not alone. It is called being human. You are allowed. You belong." Loice Swisher, MD. Clinical Associate Professor Emergency Medicine. Drexel University. Philadelphia. PA.

BECOMING A
DOCTORS' DOCTOR

Becoming a Doctors' Doctor:

A Memoir

by

Michael F Myers, MD

ISBN: 9798663704809

Table of Contents

For my patients,
with respect and gratitude

NOTE

There are many case examples from my practice in this book. With the exception of where it is written that this is a true story that has been read and approved by my patient for disclosure, including the use of pseudonyms, all are disguised and composites of many to protect the privacy of my patients.

Attempts have been made to contact the copyright holder, Physicians' Money Digest, for permission to reprint some of the case examples in Chapter Six. Sincere acknowledgment is made here for their use in this work.

Preface

"Through their professional training and socialization, then doctors frequently had come to see physicianhood as protective against illness – as immunity and defense."

Robert Klitzman, *When Doctors Become Patients* (New York: Oxford University Press, 2008) 33.

This book is one man's journey as he evolves into his life as a doctor to other doctors. More specifically, a psychiatrist to other physicians. This was not by accident. From medical school forward, I developed an interest in studying, understanding and treating the common – and not-so-common - emotional and behavioral problems that happen to us doctors. I quickly learned that we are no different than the patients we treat, a terrifying notion to most doctors, including myself. I deliberately set about acquiring the skills and, more fundamentally, the mental framework, for engendering trust and confidence in physicians who came my way.

Becoming a patient can be agonizing for physicians. For any serious illness, not simply psychiatric ones. Our training exposes us to some terrifying conditions, illnesses with grueling treatment protocols that, in seconds, can strip us of our doctor shield. Writing about his metastatic throat cancer, Dr. Eric Manheimer put it crisply: "No amount of doctoring can prepare you for being a patient."[1]

For many people, the thought of a physician having personal problems is alien, even heresy. We are seen as above or immune to the vulnerabilities and flaws of the rest of humankind. Doctors are revered as highly-educated professionals, solid as a rock, healers driven by an immutable code who can be counted on to take care of us when we're sick, applying their wisdom and medical or surgical prowess to make us better - even to save our lives in times of crisis. But we're not perfect, as we too can get ill and need colleagues to help us in our hour of need, and that is where I come in. Doctors do not go easily into that state we call in medicine "the patient role." They don't call their primary care doctor - most don't even have one - to book an early appointment. They're averse to sitting in waiting rooms because it's embarrassing and they feel diminished; even passing a written prescription to a pharmacist – and scanning her face for surprise or judgment as she reads it – can be awkward. They feel self-conscious that they need a "biological fix" because they've been betrayed by their body – or even worse – their mind.

In my practice, I saw far too many physicians who delayed coming to see me and were much worse for it. Their worry, irritability, tattered thinking, despondent mood or overuse of drugs or alcohol had spilled into their work, prompting the nurses and other doctors to question their safety and competence with patients. Others were not compromised at work, but their symptoms and actions had eroded or destroyed their loving relationships at home. Not only was this unfortunate – and sad - but these doctors were harder to treat and took longer to recover. When I learned of a colleague who had taken her own life in the mid-1980s – and reportedly refused all help for her severe mood swings – I was shaken. And determined. I decided then and there to focus even more on fighting the ever-present barriers that physicians – and the medical culture – erect to timely and lifesaving psychiatric treatment. The next day I decided to restrict my private practice to medical students and physicians – and their families. As of this writing, I've treated more than seven-hundred as patients, and continue to consult on many other doctors referred to me for expert opinion.

As the title implies, *Becoming a Doctors' Doctor: A Memoir* is a dynamic endeavor. My journey has been decades in duration and continues to evolve. I have been immeasurably changed by the work and continue to be enriched daily. Treating troubled physicians and learning from them has ignited me to my core. I have always worn many hats – clinician, teacher, researcher, writer, committee person, medical leader, volunteer and advocate. Every one of these facets of my professional being has been shaped and refined by my physician patients and their loved ones. All psychiatrists are privy to the most private of matters, and to the panoply of thoughts, emotions and conflicts of our patients. Having a lens into the heart and soul of physicians has been a gift. Creating a safe place for them to yield their doctor persona and tackle their insecurities, abuse, shame, guilt, rage, betrayal, fraudulent feelings, despair, loneliness, suicidal urges, acceptance – and yes, joy – enables this process. It is my brand. Helping others helps others, and in the end, healthier doctors provide more authentic care to their patients.

Enjoy the ride. And for the young reader, especially if you're a medical student or early career physician, I hope that my story inspires you to lend a hand to a medical colleague in need. Even once helps.

References

1. Eric Manheimer, "When Doctors Become Patients." *New York Times* Editorial. September 3, 2011.

Introduction

Christmas day 1970. I am in my second year of residency training in psychiatry and on call at Vancouver General Hospital. I'm greeted cheerily – and a bit wearily - by the psych nurse in our emergency room: "Good morning doctor, we've got a very nice Christmas present for you. A patient in Quiet Room 3. Totally in 'la-la land'. He thinks he's a doctor and insists we call him Dr. Monroe. The PRN Chlorpromazine ain't touching him – one bit." I have a quick look at his hospital chart. He was brought in by the police from the airport after he was removed from an aircraft for threatening a flight attendant who refused to serve him more alcohol. The report reads "Won't stop talking, cursing, uncooperative, needs to be restrained." The notes from the emergency physician and admitting nurse are brief but clear, summarized as "Has been drinking, belligerent, rambling speech, wants to be released. Vital signs normal."

As I head toward Dr. Monroe's room, I hear a man's voice bellowing – and murdering – the popular seasonal song "Jingle Bell Rock." I see Ralph, the weathered psych aide whom I've come to know over the past few weeks, standing outside Quiet Room 3. His smile always lights up the room but he's in especially good form this morning. I grin too, and we shake our heads in unison. It's the familiar nonverbal connection between mental health professionals – part of the affectionate code of our craft and always a reminder. A reminder of why we do what we do, our calling to help folks who are struggling with states of mind so distinct from usual, and mostly painful and frightening, if not to themselves then certainly to their families and others who care about and love them. Ralph unlocks the door, I introduce myself to Dr. Monroe and ask if I can come in. Our work begins.

His symptoms and behavioral changes all added up to mania. When I presented him to my attending psychiatrist who agreed with the "slam dunk" bipolar diagnosis, he asked me if I had certified him yet. I said: "No" and he said: "Why not?" I hesitated. He said: "What's wrong?" I murmured something like: "But he's a doctor." The attending said: "So what – if he weren't a physician, would you have certified him?" I immediately said: "Of course, he's really, really sick - and high risk." He looked at me with a wise smile and said: "Go get the pink papers." Teaching moment never to be forgotten. Don't treat doctor patients any differently than others. Little did I know that this action on his part would be the harbinger of an amazing career looking after physicians. But I struggled with his admonition that doctor-patients are the same as everyone else - most of the time I got it right, but not always, as will become clear throughout this book.

I finished my residency training in 1972, but my plans to open a private practice were dashed because I failed my specialty examinations. Fortunately, I was able to find a job working on an inpatient psychiatric unit at the University of British Columbia's

Shaughnessy Veteran's Hospital in Vancouver. Not only did this help me pay the bills, but it also enabled me to improve my knowledge and confidence so that I passed the boards the second time around with no difficulty. I quickly found an office, hired a secretary, and launched my half-time practice in Vancouver. The remainder of the week I continued my work at Shaughnessy, looking after seriously-ill inpatients, and teaching medical students and residents in both psychiatry and family medicine.

I loved being in private practice, and from the beginning I was referred and began to look after physicians. Fortunately, I didn't find this as intimidating as most other young psychiatrists, in part because I had learned so much looking after Dr. Monroe, not just in the emergency room but after I'd admitted him to our inpatient unit. I spent a great deal of time with him, especially after his psychotic symptoms abated, and he opened up to me. I was fascinated by his journey into medical school, given that he had come from such a troubled and deprived background. He had tremendous ambition and commitment to serving others, and I was moved by his empathy for his patients. His personal woundedness propelled him to make life better for others. When his wife and children flew into town and arrived at the hospital, I marveled at my clinical supervisor's actions. He put us all together in a conference room – Dr. Monroe, Mrs. Monroe, their two teenagers, myself and him – and explained what was happening. With compassion, clinical savvy and confidence he converted a frightful and confusing situation into one of hope and certainty. I was dazzled.

But I too was on a journey. Dr. Monroe and my supervisor were two of the defining people I met along the way.

Shaped by an Indelible Memory

My mother is lying motionless on the kitchen floor, on her stomach, as if she's napping. It's wintertime on my family's farm in Chatham, Ontario, a school night, around 5 o'clock. I'm 12 years old, and I've just come into the house after feeding my chickens. I'm shocked and terrified. I'm down on my knees shaking her shoulder and calling to her: "Mom, are you okay? Can you hear me?" She stirs slightly but doesn't open her eyes or say anything. But I know she's alive. My father is out of town, my two older brothers are away at boarding school. I call out to my younger sister Penny and little brother John who have been playing in the basement. They stay at her side. I run to the phone and call my aunt who lives about a mile away on another farm. She is there in a few minutes and takes charge. My mother begins to wake up but is groggy as my aunt and I help her get up. We walk her to the bedroom and my aunt asks me to leave, that she'll stay with my mother. "You go finish making dinner and feed Penny and John."

Later that evening my dad arrived home from his business trip. He talks to my aunt who has come out of the bedroom. Their voices are low but I learn that my mother is fine, and that she's sleeping now. My aunt leaves and I warm up a leftover dinner for my father. Penny and John are in their bedrooms doing homework, so dad and I are alone. He sits at the table reading the paper, not talking. I ask: "What's wrong with mom? Is she going to be okay?" He looks at me briefly and says: "Oh, nothing to worry about, your mother just had too much to drink. She'll be fine. Thanks for calling Aunt Charlotte. You better get to your homework now, Michael." He returned to his newspaper and nothing more was said.

From that day on I became a hawk. I quickly learned that my mother had a drinking problem and no one in our family wanted to talk about it. When I told my two older brothers Paul and Peter about Mom passing out they were blasé. They told me that this had been going on for a while. They reminisced with me about a couple of family events – the previous Christmas and a summer picnic – when my mother was slurring her words and not making much sense – and my father quietly explaining that she wasn't feeling well so was going to lie down. These – and many other unusual times – now made more sense to me. My statements to my brothers like: "But why doesn't dad do something? Like take her to the doctor?" were useless. They weren't prepared to say anything and I felt dismissed just like I felt with my father's words "She'll be fine." What's worse is that within a year or so they were doing a lot of drinking themselves and getting into trouble at school.

Several months later, I sat on the edge of my seat in school assembly when our principal invited a speaker from Alcoholics Anonymous to address us. He told us all about the symptoms and signs of alcoholism, how it affects the family, and what AA has to offer. I furtively grabbed two pamphlets after the lecture and stuffed them in my school bag. That evening I planted one in the top drawer of each of my parents' bureaus. I was shaking with nerves. What I was doing felt right but yet wrong. First, because their bedroom and especially their bureaus were private and I felt I was trespassing and violating their adult space. Second, I sensed that my message wasn't the natural order of things, that parents confront and reach out to their kids, not the other way around. I had never done anything so brazen before. Would they be angry? Would I be punished?

I waited and waited – and waited some more. For weeks. Nothing happened, and nothing was said about AA, but I was changed forever. I knew then that we had a shameful family secret that no one was even prepared to address, and that I was on my own. My vigilance was in full swing. My mother had a drinking ritual. She spent much of her time reading in her bedroom. She would emerge, pass through the living room to the empty kitchen, run the water at the kitchen sink, take a glass from the cupboard, quickly pour a shot of rye whiskey from the bottle on the shelf below, run water into the glass, cup it under her arm inside her cardigan sweater and walk carefully back through the living room to her bedroom. I got so I didn't need to see this over the years, I could hear it, and I hated it – and hated her. My unhappiness and resentment built, and I couldn't wait to graduate from school and go off to college.

A few years later, I learned that a segment of medical students grow up in homes where one or both parents struggle with alcohol or other forms of substance use. And I began to see how lonely my mother was. And how much she had sacrificed in her marriage. She was typical of the 1950's housewife but instead of taking the nerve pill, meprobamate ("mother's little helper"), she turned to alcohol. It would still be almost a decade before Betty Friedan's *The Feminine Mystique*[1] shook up the prevailing norms of middle-class households, and women began to reclaim their voices.

References

1. Betty Friedan, *The Feminine Mystique.* (New York: WW Norton & Company. 1963)

Chapter One

Looking Back to Go Forward

"The gap between what we know and what we aim for persists. And this gap complicates everything we do."

Atul Gawande, *Complications: A Surgeon's Notes on an Imperfect Science*. (London: Picador, 2003) 7.

My First Exposure to Psychiatry

Despite my excitement in the previous pages, looking back I realize that becoming a psychiatrist was never one of my original career choices. In fact, for certain reasons, I was a relatively late bloomer into the field. I studied medicine in the early- to mid-1960s, and Psychiatry as a specialty in many medical centers was not ranked as highly as, for example, Surgery, Internal Medicine, Obstetrics and Gynecology, or Pediatrics. This was rooted in stigma. Psychiatric patients were viewed with judgment, anxiety and gross misunderstanding. They were marginalized - housed in state or provincial mental hospitals, often at a distance from the vibrant learning opportunities of general hospitals - and acute psychiatric units in general hospitals were relatively new as teaching sites. But not just the patients were stigmatized, psychiatrists were as well. They were typecast in various ways: not real doctors; not that smart and thus in psychiatry by default; weird or oddball like their patients; or mentally unstable and at risk of breaking down and killing themselves. Overall, not a pretty picture.

But let me be more specific about my training and exposure to psychiatry as a medical student. At my medical school - the University of Western Ontario in London, Ontario - Psychiatry was not a particularly long-established, ample or strong department; it did not even stand alone, rather was shared with Preventive Medicine in terms of departmental leadership and authority. There were a small handful of professors who taught us, all white males. The lectures were excellent, however, and I found learning about such things as schizophrenia, manic-depressive illness and depression interesting and captivating. One of our best teachers did in fact border on the stereotype of being an eccentric, but in a charming and delightful way - he smoked in class, as many professors did in that era before the 1964 Surgeon General's Report, but eccentrically held his cigarette between his fourth and fifth fingers. I enjoyed psychiatry equally to all the other fields we were studying, and my vision of it was inclusive, insofar as our own patients belonged in the house of medicine as much as middle-aged men with chest pain, women in labor, or children struggling with asthma.

I remember one patient with clarity even after all these years. She was a college student who had been admitted involuntarily to the acute psychiatric unit of Victoria Hospital, where I was doing my clerkship. She had been in the hospital for about a week when I started, and my supervisor assigned her to me on the first day. His policy was for all new students to simply go have a chat with the patient and when finished sit down with him and the other students to share our impressions. We had never observed a patient being interviewed before and were absolute rookies. He was aware of this, and his modus operandi was for us to have initial exposure to a psychiatric inpatient before we learned and observed certain basic skills. My patient was intelligent, articulate and intriguing, and I didn't have to ask her any questions - she opened up and told me all about herself, that her roommate and parents had panicked and called 911, that she really wasn't hearing voices, that it was true her landlord had wiretapped their apartment and was recording their conversations, that her boyfriend and her roommate were indeed sleeping together and she had proof of that. Her story unraveled with animation and precision, but after an hour of this, I realized I needed to say goodbye to her and report to my peers and supervisor. The long and the short of it was that I believed everything she said to me. In fact, when I spoke in the case conference, I told my supervisor that there had been an awful mistake, that she wasn't ill and didn't need to be in the hospital. What I will never forget is how he accepted my account without judgment and simply said: "Thank you. Let's all go to her room and get this sorted out." I watched carefully as he interviewed her. Fortunately, she couldn't see my jaw drop as her psychosis poured forth in technicolor for all to see – nor did he shame me when we returned to the conference room to discuss her diagnosis of paranoid schizophrenia and its treatment.

I won the prize for earning the highest grade in psychiatry that year, the only academic accolade I garnered in medical school. But my reaction was strange. I was proud but I diminished its importance both to myself and to others. I stated that my preceptor was a pushover and gave inflated grades. I felt that it was an easy exam and I was simply lucky to ace it. Years later, after the 1970s-era term "imposter syndrome" was no longer confined to women, could I see that I had vestiges of it myself at that time. I also think that I had internalized much of the societal stigma attached to psychiatry, that yes, I won this prize, but it was no big deal - it was in psychiatry, not in something meritorious like surgery or internal medicine. I graduated from medical school with no instinctive sense that I might actually have a proficiency in psychiatry and should consider specializing in it. That decision came two-and-a-half years later.

Tragedy Struck

Before coming to that, I need to look back even further in time, to an event in my life that paradoxically attracted me to psychiatry but pushed me away at the same time. It was the fall of 1962 and I was a first-year medical student. I had been home visiting my parents over the Thanksgiving weekend, and at the end of my return drive pulled up to park my car in front of my apartment in London, Ontario, one I shared with three other medical students. It was Monday October 8th at around 8pm. Our landlady was standing at the front entrance, and she looked tense and distraught as she asked me to come into her apartment for a few minutes. She told me to sit down and said: "I have sad news to tell you. It's about your roommate Bill. His parents called a couple of hours ago. They said he won't be coming back to medical school. He died over the weekend. They said it was suicide." I was stunned and felt sick to my stomach.

Bill was found dead in his car, parked on a lonely stretch of beach, with a hose running from the exhaust pipe into its interior. Although I didn't know him all that well, he and I often studied together and quizzed each other in anatomy. I didn't see it coming. My mind went into overdrive. What did he mean on Wednesday night – the last I saw him alive – when he said: "See you after the weekend"? Was there a kind of cryptic message? Was he depressed, desperate? Did his face look different or his voice sound tentative?

The next morning, Tuesday October 9th, at the beginning of our first class, I asked our Biochemistry professor if I could make a brief announcement before he began. I will never forget standing in front of my classmates and delivering them the news. I remember my wobbly knees and quivering voice. I especially recall scanning their faces – they were frozen and shocked. I told my classmates I would keep them updated as I learned more and then returned to my seat. No one spoke a word. The professor broke the silence and awkwardly said: "So let's return to the Krebs cycle."

But I never learned more. I phoned Bill's parents and asked about the funeral. His father was kind but curt, and said that it was a private matter and thanked me for calling. There was no information from the Dean's office, and no reaching out. No one spoke to our class, and we did not send flowers or a card to the family - it was almost as if Bill had never existed. I look back and think - with much shame - how disrespectful, and how different things would have been if he'd died in a car accident.

Expanding My Horizons

During my third year of medical school I applied for a summer externship in Internal Medicine at Mount Sinai Hospital in Minneapolis. I was restless and wanted to get a taste of how medicine was taught and practiced in the United States, and I was overjoyed when I received their letter of acceptance. The memories I have of July and August of 1965 are rich and warm. I expanded my knowledge of clinical medicine and gained confidence in my diagnostic and procedural skills. I met medical students, residents and staff physicians from all over the country and beyond, and loved the cultural diversity of this beautiful city. I also gained exposure to underserved and indigent patients in our teaching at Hennepin County General Hospital in downtown Minneapolis, which proved significant. I was struck by the medical complexity of these patients, their unvarnished environmental circumstances, their fortitude and, most important, their dignity. I returned to Canada with my heart set on entering the US matching system so that I could pursue my postgraduate training in a large urban public setting. I applied to Bellevue Hospital in New York City, Cook County Hospital in Chicago, Charity Hospital in New Orleans and Los Angeles County General Hospital in Los Angeles.

But something else was driving this big decision. I was running away – from my small town, my family, my religion, and the comfort of my homogeneous culture. As I look back on that time in my life, through the lens of a psychiatrist, I can say boldly that I didn't know myself terribly well - or, to use the language of psychiatry, I didn't have much real insight into who I was or what made me tick. All I knew was that I craved adventure and exposure to the world beyond southern Ontario, and that I was in deficit mode - needing to make up for lost time, viewing my life theretofore as restrictive, unenlightened, provincial and mundane.

I graduated from the University of Western Ontario Medical School in May of 1966 and headed out to California to begin my internship at Los Angeles County General Hospital-USC Medical Center. This was a rotating internship and a busy but exciting year. Despite Bill's death by suicide four years earlier, the subject of physician health or illness was nowhere on my radar. But late in the year, I remember coming upon a small huddle of my fellow interns one morning, and I asked them what was going on. They told me a story about an anesthesiology resident who had tried to kill herself over the weekend. She lived in the same interns building as I did but we had never met. That Sunday evening, she had started an intravenous drip in one of her arm veins to which she added barbiturates; she then woke up the following morning, groggy but still alive, got dressed, and walked over to our hospital's emergency room and asked to talk to a psychiatrist.

What I will never forget is the tone of the huddle. My intern buddies were telling this story in such a mean-spirited, gossipy and immature way – and even joked about what kind of a doctor can't even kill herself properly. I recognized this as gallows hu-mor, code in medicine, especially when trainees are exhausted or overwhelmed by the awful truth of life's horrors. My reaction was different – shock and disbelief at first, but as I left them to start my work I mused, how sad and lonely she must have felt. Not just while she was arranging to kill herself, but also when she woke up *all alone,* still alive, and then walking *all alone* to that emergency room to ask for help. I remember flashing back to Bill and thinking the same thoughts about him, how lonely and alone he must have felt, and the muted, obtuse reaction to his suicide. Then it dawned on me, and I saw the parallel in these two tragedies, and how psychiatric crises are different from other medical events. If the anesthesiology resident had fallen and hurt her leg, or suddenly developed a blinding headache, she would have reached out to someone for help, rather than having to cope with her pain all alone. For a physical injury she would have received medical attention and relief; for psychic pain things are not that simple.

I finished my internship at USC at the end of June 1967 and decided to take time off from my medical work and go traveling overseas for a few months. I was exhausted and needed a break from the rigor. Although I had secured a residency in Internal Medicine back in Canada which was to begin July 1st, I had let them know a few months earlier that I'd changed my mind. This was a competitive residency and they were gracious in ac-cepting my decision, even inviting me to apply again in another year or two, should I still be considering that field. After my sojourn through Europe, I moved to Michigan and started to work as an Emergency physician at Detroit Receiving Hospital in October of 1967. The hours there were long, and I worked nonstop from start to finish, running from one life-threatening situation to another. The litany of woes included individuals with heart attacks, asthmatic attacks, withdrawal from alcohol and other drugs, heroin overdoses, diabetic coma patients, gunshot wounds, stabbings, sexual assaults, frostbitten limbs and gangrene in the homeless, lacerated wrists and other crises in the mentally ill.

But again, the matter of physician health or wellness was not on my mind until one Monday morning in January or February of 1968 at the start of my shift, when a young man shuffled – I mean that literally – shuffled up to me and introduced himself as my new intern for the month – I'll call him Dr. Smith. I tried to get past his appearance – he was stiff, his hands were trembling and his face was immobile as I proceeded to orient him to the ER. I assigned him a patient to work up – a man with chest pain, as I recall – and told him to grab me when he was done so I could go over his findings and discuss treatment. I began seeing other patients, but soon noticed he didn't return to me in a timely manner. I went to look for him and found him at the patient's bedside, just sitting there, as if he were a silent visitor. The patient, fortunately, was napping despite the surrounding din, and didn't seem to notice. I went with Dr. Smith to a side room to have him present his findings on the patient, and that's when I noticed he was drooling saliva and his speech was slurred. I realized then that this poor guy was not well. I asked him if he was okay, and he told me that he'd been diagnosed with depression and was seeing a psychiatrist; he also wondered if he might be having side effects to one of his medications. I certainly didn't know much about psychiatric drugs in those days, but offered to call his psychiatrist for him, which I did. His doctor wanted to see him straightaway, and fortunately his office was just across the street, and so off he went. I never saw him again, and a different intern appeared that afternoon.

As I write these words "I never saw him again" it drives home to me how silenced we were about psychiatric illness in doctors in 1968. I want to believe that I would have followed up if his diagnosis was lymphoma - that I would have asked around, called the internship training director, or visited him or sent a card. At least I hope I would have.

I left my position in Detroit toward the end of June that year and returned to Los Angeles County General Hospital-USC Medical Center to begin my internal medicine residency on July 1,1968. Seven to eight months into my residency was when I made the decision to leave internal medicine at the end of that year and begin to train in psychiatry. Let me explain how that evolved.

Choosing Psychiatry

I started internal medicine with enthusiasm. I enjoyed working hard, treating patients and teaching medical students and interns. Having interned at Los Angeles County-USC Medical Center - known colloquially as Mother County - I had a leg up. I was familiar with the physical layout of one of the largest public hospitals and medical training centers in the United States, as well as the ethos and system of care there for the indigent population of the Los Angeles area. I also knew a number of the other residents and clinical supervisors, which matters when you're in training because the hours are long, and you're exposed to substantial levels of severe illness and trauma, both physical and psychological. It's comforting to have colleagues to talk to, and let off steam with, and you never feel alone.

But after about six months of this, I began to feel something was missing, though at the time I couldn't quite put my finger on it. After a series of general medicine rotations, I started an elective in gastroenterology. This was a game changer. Enter Dr. Bill Kiely, psychiatrist and chief of the consultation service to medicine. I had never met a physician, let alone a psychiatrist, like him before this time. He appeared on the ward, asked me to summarize my patients, then said: "Let's go meet these fine folks and I'll see if I can help." We walked together into the multi-bedded room and the first thing he looked for was two chairs so that both he and I could take a seat by the patient's bedside. What this magnificent man taught me is best conveyed by three pivotal takeaways.

First, yes, we're the doctors here and we need to figure out what's wrong and fix things, but in order to do that we should be at the patient's level, not standing over and looking down on them and making them feel more diminished than they already are by laying sick in their bed.

Second, start your initial encounter with your patient by asking an open-ended question beyond: "What brings you to the hospital today?" or: "How are you feeling this morning?" Instead, Dr. Kiely would ask: "Tell me about yourself…" All of my patients were stunned by this question and would respond with a frown or a gesture of "huh?" to which he would say: "Let me help you. I'd like to get to know you a little bit. Can you tell me what you do for a living?" But then he waited for a response before asking the next question, then waited again. He talked to my patients as if he had all the time in the world. They opened up about what was going on in their lives before they started to get the awful cramping in their bellies or bloody diarrhea or vomiting or high fever and sweating, common medical symptoms of GI distress.

And third, that your patients are much more than their medical symptoms. You have to understand the context of their lives and how much factors like fractious or distant relationships with family members, unemployment, loneliness, religion, ethnicity, trauma and so forth round out the picture. You need to treat the patient, not just the signs and symptoms of their illness.

I then was able to pinpoint what was missing in my training and the source of my frustration. Not only was this kind of psycho-social thinking rather foreign in internal medicine training of the 1960s, but it was almost impossible to put into action. There was no time, and you'd never be able to move onto your next patient, who was often critically ill and emergent. You needed to ask rapid-fire questions, complete your physical examination and get on with your treatment plan.

In addition to this gnawing feeling that I've just explained, there was another thing on my mind, and this was not a complaint about internal medicine, indeed just the opposite. It was internal medicine that exposed me to suicide, more precisely, patients who had attempted suicide, and I learned how to treat them and often save their lives. But still, there were too many times where we didn't save their lives, and this troubled me.

I treated many patients who had made serious suicide attempts. Overdoses of powerful sleeping medications and other barbiturates were not uncommon and lethal in high doses, and many of these patients died under my watch in our medical intensive care units without ever regaining consciousness. But despite my limited understanding of suicide in those days, and my busyness with treating my patients' catastrophic medical problems, I struggled with the "whys" – why would such a beautiful young person want to die? What was so wrong with their life? Why do people lose hope? Walking out of the ICU into the waiting room and talking to their anguished relatives – their girlfriend or husband or mom or dad – was tough, and I had minimal training in this most vital dimension of being a doctor, the art of medicine. I was fortunate to have a number of compassionate attending physicians who were my role models. Their gift was helping me say: "I'm sorry… Sandra's coma has deepened overnight and her blood pressure is falling" or "I'm very sorry… your husband died a few minutes ago… I'm sorry."

I realized that training in psychiatry would give me the opportunity to understand suicide far better, and hopefully allow me to make a difference at an earlier stage. My exposure to psychiatry in medical school was clearly not enough. I was ill-equipped to fully grasp when individuals begin to have thoughts of suicide and when those thoughts progress into planning or researching methods – and then acting on them. As I thought back to the numbers of dead-on-arrival patients that I attended to in Detroit – dead by overdoses, self-inflicted gunshot wounds or stabbings, electrocution, asphyxia, drowning or jumping from tall buildings – I knew that I wanted to do more than pronounce people and fill out death certificates. Becoming a psychiatrist could help me save some of these despairing souls.

And maybe I might figure out why Bill killed himself.

Training in Psychiatry

Although I had the option of simply switching out of Internal Medicine residency and applying to Psychiatry residency at Los Angeles County-USC Medical Center, I only had two more years on my study visa - this was not enough time to complete my training in Psychiatry, so I applied to the residency program at the University of British Columbia in Vancouver. I had never traveled to western Canada before, so moving and studying there appealed to my adventuresome spirit. Also, this was during the height of the Vietnam War, and Vancouver was becoming a major haven for young folks fleeing the US. Many of our newly-acquired friends in the city were conscientious objectors and draft evaders.

From the beginning I enjoyed studying psychiatry. My residency years spanned the late 1960s and early 1970s, an eventful time in our world and in my chosen field. In my first year, I quickly realized that I had much to learn about the nuts and bolts of basic psychiatry. My chief resident was great - he was patient with me, gave me extra supervision, and most important, he used humor

with aplomb while pointing out my mistakes when I was interviewing patients. And there was a good amount of training that
I had to unlearn. When seeing patients, I needed to slow down,
listen more, listen carefully, talk less, stop interrogating and let
my caring come through. He kept reminding me that I wasn't
working in the emergency room or intensive care unit anymore,
and that skills essential there were importantly different than
ones we use in psychiatry. I remember writing to a friend that
year, and telling him that I had found my bliss in psychiatry.

In what ways did my residency set me on the path of becoming
a doctors' doctor? Primarily, it was because I had increasing
exposure to treating doctors and their families. I looked after
the wife of a physician who was hospitalized for severe depression, which was then known as involutional melancholia. She
had taken an overdose of sleeping pills but called for help before
suffering any toxic effects. A fulltime homemaker and mother,
she fell into a severe depression during her menopausal years,
when the last of her four daughters went off to college. The details of treatment are not as important as her VIP status on the
unit, because her husband was the chair of a branch of medicine
at our medical school. The nurses, medical students and other
team members seemed intimidated by her, and kind of fussed
around in a bit of a dither. What was clear – and what I learned
from her – was how wrong all of this was. She was the last one
to expect or demand preferential status. She was a modest and
understated woman who had lost her core identity many years
earlier when she left practicing law to devote her energies to
being a mother and a doctor's wife. Now, she was bereft and
rudderless - her kids were no longer dependent upon her, and

her husband was busy with his career and rarely at home. She wondered if life was worth continuing. An antidepressant medication, supportive talking, and group therapy were especially helpful, and her mood began to improve, in part due to several sessions that my supervisor and I had with her and her husband when he came to visit. I learned valuable lessons from the two of them, mostly about how vulnerable they felt and just how much they each wanted help - not entitlement, and not a kid-gloves approach.

While training in child and adolescent psychiatry, a faculty member invited me to treat, under his fine tutelage, a 17-year-old woman with anorexia nervosa. I'll call her Ann. Her parents were both physicians and they and their daughter all consented to this arrangement. My supervisor was extremely busy with his academic work and an overflowing private practice, and I think this is why Ann's parents went along with her becoming a "teaching case" who might actually get more intensive treatment by a supervised greenhorn than with him. I was intimidated, but this lessened as I got to know Ann better, and participated in family sessions where I observed her mom and dad. I saw them simply as worried and confused parents - the fact that they were physicians was irrelevant. Another wonderful lesson for me. I was pleased that they seemed to find my suggestions about ways of coping with anxiety around family mealtimes actually helpful.

These are all clinical examples of how my preparedness for looking after doctors and their families got started, but alongside this was the fact that I was also maturing in my personal life. When I finished training and opened my private practice, I had been married for four years, and was the father of a two-year-old. I was now, by virtue of my own life experience, equipped with some of the same growing pains that doctor patients bring to psychiatrists when seeking treatment. I was not just "talking the talk" but beginning to "walk the walk," and the inevitable challenges and wonders of my professional and personal life were giving me a more thoughtful, empathic and realistic perspective to helping others.

Chapter Two

The Early Years of Clinical Practice

I was in private practice from 1973 until 2008, and always half time; the rest of each week I worked at one or more of our university teaching hospitals, where I taught psychiatry to medical students and residents in both psychiatry and family medicine. Most of this was clinical bedside teaching on inpatients, outpatients and consulting to other branches of medicine. As I look back on those years, I recall how much I enjoyed having these two dimensions in my career. Very different endeavors but equally fulfilling. I seemed to have the best of two worlds.

A Medical Student in Crisis

The following is a true story that has been read and approved by my patient for disclosure.

It's 6pm Tuesday September 25,1973. A third-year medical student, I'll call him Adam, and I have just finished seeing my last patient in my office. We're done for the day — and this is also Adam's last session, as he's in the final week of his clerkship in psychiatry. He says to me: "Got a few minutes, Dr. Myers?" I look at him and his face is not the same as it was a few minutes earlier, the face I've been seeing all afternoon, the familiar look of the keen and engaged medical trainee. He is pale and frightened looking, blank and distant. I say: "Of course, sit down, what's going on?" He starts, slowly and with hesitation: "I'm depressed, like really depressed. I've been going up and down and slowly getting worse and worse for about a year but it's gotten bad since the weekend." I instinctively switch roles from being his teacher, which I've been doing for the past four hours, to being his doctor. I hear myself uttering the familiar refrain of therapists: "Tell me more about that…" That invitation and a few direct questions open a floodgate of pain and misery.

Adam was 23 years old. He told me he was fine until toward the end of his first year of medical school. He was living with his fiancée, and things in general seemed to be okay, but he began to have trouble sleeping and never felt rested during the day. His mood and thoughts changed — he used words like "emptiness inside," "there's a dullness," "I'm finished," "I feel useless, I'm a failure, I'm taking up a place in medical school," "my self-esteem is down, so is my self-confidence," and "all of this gets worse and eats away at me as the day goes on." I probed and learned that he could hardly concentrate on his studies and his grades were falling. He was withdrawing from his classmates and friends, craved time alone, and had lost his interest in sports. This only compounded his sense of alienation from his medical school peers and made him doubt his quest to become a doctor. And he had no energy, he felt "old." Through the course of this, not only did his engagement break off, but even a recent relationship with a classmate went south. He had no hope that he could ever become who he was before. He confided in me that ten days earlier, while visiting his parents for the weekend, he'd put his father's grouse-hunting shotgun in the trunk of his car, "just in case I need it." My *follow-up questions about this all pointed in one direction - that Adam was at high risk of suicide.*

The good news was that I didn't have to wrestle with him to convince him that he needed to come into the hospital. I think he was too spent, too weakened, too forlorn to fight. The bad news was that I was leaving the next day on a two-week vacation. Fortunately, I found a bed for him that evening, got him admitted directly from my office, and did all of the admission work myself. The staff psychiatrist, whom I knew, looked after him — superbly — while I was gone. When I returned, I was able to visit him regularly on the unit over the third week of his hospitalization, and assist with his transition from inpatient care to my office. He was not out of the woods yet by any means, but he was no longer suicidal, and the physical and biological symptoms of his depression were almost entirely gone. He returned to school, and over the next few weeks regained his commitment to study, including his feeling of belonging in medicine.

Adam and I met regularly for medication monitoring and psychotherapy, at first weekly, and then every two weeks. The specifics and details are less important than the process itself. He allowed himself to be cared for, something that medical students and physicians struggle with, as most are masters at caring for their patients but resist others caring for them. He had deep-seated problems with his self-esteem that went back to his childhood. He loved his father, but his dad was tough, an old country taskmaster and disciplinarian. As a result, Adam had become a young man who was anxious, ambitious and striving but quite hard on himself, a perfectionist and guilt-prone doctor in-the-making. An added major stressor in his life began five years earlier when he was in college. His mother developed a brain tumor, and although she survived neurosurgery, she was unable to function as she once did, and had had two psychiatric hospitalizations since for suicidal depression. The mother he once knew and loved was gone, a loss that he was only now becoming conscious of. He did his best to avoid thinking about her by focusing intently on his studies while competing to get into medical school.

Adam also struggled in his relationships with women. More about this as the narrative continues. My last visit with him was on May 7, 1974. He had started his final year of medical school, was off his antidepressant medication, and his mood was stable. It was several years before I saw him again, specifically October 16,1991, and this time he came with his wife for marital therapy. They had been married for four years, and had two children of their own and two children from his wife's first marriage. She was being treated for depression by her primary care physician. They were arguing frequently and having trouble communicating, which was getting both of them down and upsetting their children. After meeting with each of them alone to get more personal details, we started couples therapy, but only met for one visit before they dropped out. I heard nothing until Adam called and booked an urgent visit with me years later on April 29,1999. He began the session with these words: "The last few years have been a living hell." He and his wife had recently separated and were filing for divorce, and he was back on antidepressant medication from his primary care physician, which was easing this stressful transition in his life. Colleagues at work were worried about him and whether he was fit to practice. I agreed with their concerns and put him on medical leave until his confidence returned.

Adam and I began to meet on a regular basis again so that I could be a support to him and oversee his medication, which became complicated because he developed side-effects. While trying other antidepressants, his mood worsened and he developed suicidal thinking. Fortunately, I was able to find a psychiatrist closer to home for him whom he could see on a more frequent basis. This — and regular visits with a psychologist — worked, and he regained his equilibrium.

As an aside, when I reached out to Adam in the summer of 2019 to acquire his consent for publishing his story, he added the following piece in his email reply to me that speaks to the awkwardness and discomfort about mental illness in the world of medicine twenty years ago:

"Later in 1999, I returned to work after three months of medical leave, stabilization on medication and ongoing sessions with my psychiatrist as well as counselling with a local psychologist. The medical community where I worked was fairly close knit, consisting of ten surgeons, two internists and twenty-six family physicians, and we all knew each other professionally, mingled regularly in the Hospital medical lounge, as well as socially. All of the surgeons and specialists were male. In the first week back in the OR many female nurses sympathetically asked how I was doing, for which I was most grateful. Of the physicians, only two men approached me in private, enquired how I was coping and expressed concern for me. Both put a hand on my shoulder or arm. Those brief, simple gestures of touch and conversation meant so much to me at the time, knowing that a colleague cared and was concerned. Each episode resulted in an immediate, and overwhelming inner flood of emotion, of release, suddenly almost crying with relief. But of course, men don't cry. Since then I have actually allowed myself to shed a tear on occasion."

I did not see Adam again until January 17, 2008. The backstory was that he had moved to a different city and relocated professionally at the same time. He had stayed on his medication, and although his personal and professional life remained challenging, he was coping much better. He had been in a stable relationship for a couple of years and because of common sexual side-effects he wondered about a change of medication. He went to his primary care physician and with his blessing began gradually tapering his medication. Unfortunately, within a few weeks he got sick again. His words were: "I've had a big relapse. I'm having trouble coping with everything in my life." I was relieved that he'd called me, but what was so striking when he came into my office is that he looked and sounded exactly like the medical student who had reached out to me decades earlier in 1973 - just an older version of the same lost, frightened, despairing man. He had become suicidal again but he now had the insight to no longer see that as a valid option. Simply restarting his antidepressant and adding a newer medication for his obsessive thinking gave him relief. I saw him a few more times before I retired from practice and referred him back to his primary care physician.

Analysis

I have chosen to write about Adam because his story so vividly illustrates the thesis of *Becoming a Doctors' Doctor*. I began seeing him during the early months of my clinical practice, and although there were many years when he was not under my care, our work together spanned thirty-five years. He was becoming a doctor while I was becoming a doctors' doctor, and I learned an enormous amount from him as he suffered through the many challenges in his personal and professional life, and during the times in which his depression returned.

Research estimates that roughly one quarter to a third of medical students develop symptoms of depression, including suicidal thinking, at one point or another in medical school. Many tough it out on their own, and it is not known what percentage actually accept help. Practicing physicians have higher rates of depression than those measured in the general population. Unlike Adam, some medical students have even already experienced or been treated for depression before matriculating to medical school. It is no accident that I was the one he opened up to about his feelings. First, given the stigma in medicine associated with psychiatric illness and how hard it is to trust others, including psychiatrists, with what's happening to you, many ailing medical students and most physicians are careful or strategic about whom they consult. He knew of me from lectures that I'd given to his class, but it was his preceptorship with me where, as he said, he "got to see me in action," that helped him utter the words: "Got a few minutes Dr. Myers?" Second, when you're depressed, it's hard to reach out for professional help - you feel vulnerable, frightened and unworthy, and you're often sensitive to rejection or what you might misperceive as rejection. This is partly why so many depressed people delay seeking out treatment, suffering silently, as Adam did.

It has been known for a time that many physicians and medical students do not always follow conventional routes to care. So-called "curbside consults" are common. This is when a physician stops a psychiatrist or other mental health professional in the halls of a hospital or medical center and opens up about the way they're feeling, asks for advice, wonders if they should go see someone and queries their availability. Much less common is what happens in the general population, where the depressed person goes to their primary care physician and, if necessary, is referred on to a mental health professional. Adam had a doctor at the university health service but didn't tell him about his depression. I contacted this man by telephone and mailed him a consultation letter the morning after I admitted Adam to the psychiatry unit and before I left for vacation.

Not everyone would have assessed Adam as I did in my office and then go on to become his treating psychiatrist. It was the end of the day, and I did have the option of sending him "to the nearest emergency room" - a common refrain on voice mail greetings of psychologists and psychiatrists - but my instinct was to deal myself with what I felt was a crisis. There were several reasons for my decision. I easily sensed how much it must have taken for Adam to pour his heart out to me and allow me to assess him, and the thought of making him do this again that evening with a complete stranger in the ER was morally repugnant to me. His anguish was palpable. There was no longer a conflict of interest; our teacher-student relationship had just ended moments earlier, and so it was ethically acceptable for us to enter into a doctor-patient relationship. Most important, I was very concerned that he could kill himself if I didn't facilitate a smooth transition into the hospital. Roadblocks to that level of care – or perceived roadblocks – can be deadly when a severely depressed person is not treated with compassion, clarity, and a confident plan of action.

Examination of Adam's narrative also reveals that a student of medicine can become quite ill, including hospitalization, and bounce back. This speaks to the resilience of physicians and student doctors.[1] I write this with conviction because there is so much folklore and myth about physicians who become ill in medical school or residency. These young folks are commonly terrified that they'll be kicked out of training for being ill and their dreams of medicine will be dashed. It is the rare trainee who is not able to return to medical school or residency training and complete their studies. When this happens, it's usually due to their having a treatment-resistant illness - commonly a mood disorder- that doesn't respond to conventional treatment, a severe substance use disorder with multiple relapses, or personality difficulties that preclude their accepting their illnesses and embracing appropriate treatment.

Despite his depression recurring and having a fair share of hurdles in his life, Adam has many so-called "protective factors" that have enabled him to lead a fulfilling and productive life as a medical specialist. He has a pleasing personality and is well liked by his medical colleagues, who in turn are very supportive of him. He is smart, keeps up to date in his field, and is efficient at what he does. His patients and their families like him, he has never abused alcohol or other drugs, he has interests outside of medicine, and he loves his children and has been intimately involved in their rearing. He is a good patient, knows his symptoms well, has insight into what triggers him and cooperates with treatment, including taking his medications and engaging in psychotherapy to understand himself better.

Returning to the notion of doctoring other doctors, I wrote above my thoughts about why Adam turned to me in his hour of need, but why did he contact me at those other times when he needed help – specifically in 1991, 1999 and 2008? The simplest explanation is not unique to doctor-patients, rather it's that all patients prefer to see a doctor who knows them and has been helpful to them in the past. This is especially true in psychiatry because it takes time to build a trusting and mutually respectful relationship. It's epitomized in the statement: "I don't want to start all over again with a new doctor. I don't have the time or energy for that." Another explanation is the architecture of our dyadic relationship. We are both white males and represent the traditionally dominant ethnic and gender group in medicine. And there was also not an appreciable age gap - I was 30 years old, and he was 23 when he first became my patient. Did these combined factors facilitate and sustain our professional relationship?

But could there be something else? What about belonging? This has been researched at length by professor Ezra Griffith[2], and his colleague at Yale professor Michael Rowe[3], who have each written about the notion of citizenship applied to those living with a serious mental illness. When individuals experience a life disruption as a result of a recurrence, they seek to regain lost connections in an effort to become valued community members once more. They fight to belong again. I have explored this myself in an earlier book on physician suicide when I wrote about the alienation that ailing physicians feel when they're perceived to be ostracized from the club of medicine.[4] I once interviewed a physician who was recovering from a near-lethal suicide attempt. He told me that one of the strongest – and most encouraging - voices he heard in the wake of his massive injuries and loss was that of his psychiatrist, with whom he had a longstanding relationship, that he belonged in medicine. Have I represented to Adam a steadiness, a link, a conduit back to health and reentry to a medical career at those times that he has called me?

What heightens a wish or need to belong in the house of medicine speaks to the pernicious stigma attached to mental illness in doctors. As a doctors' doctor I have spent decades listening to chilling and heartbreaking accounts of how shunned or judged my patients have felt by their peers and the institutional rules of the profession of medicine. Those of us who treat physicians have a moral responsibility to do everything in our power to fight these destructive forces by educating, advocating and working for policy change.

Broadening My Scope of Practice

One thing I learned quickly in my first few years of practice is how many individuals I saw as patients whose main problem was their marriage. There were more women than men, but that doesn't necessarily mean that more women are unhappy in their marriages. Historically, married men have not sought therapy for their marital difficulties. But that aside, I felt ill-equipped to help these unhappy folks. The psychotherapy skills I had learned in my training were largely individual ones, and simply listening to these men and women was not only unhelpful but a waste of their time and money. I needed to have training and experience in couples therapy, and so I took a few short courses and did several workshops that helped me with the basics, while also reading papers and books on various theories of marital disharmony and therapeutic strategies. But as with most things in medicine, we learn the most from our patients.

I started seeing couples and fortuitously, at the same time, learned that my colleague Dr. Ingrid Pacey was feeling the same frustration as me. We had trained together in psychiatry, and she as well was in private practice, so we made the decision to begin seeing couples together. This was a watershed moment in my professional life. For almost a decade, we did couples work together on Tuesday afternoons in our office, a different couple every hour. The clinical details of that work, presented in 1979 at the Canadian Psychiatric Association Annual Meeting, are not so relevant here, but what I learned about myself is. Our collaborative co-therapist work, as a male and female psychiatrist pair, was an enduring component of my evolving feminism.

Few men called themselves feminists in the 1970s. A chance encounter sealed that for me. I met Dr. Margaret Mead at a psychiatry conference in Brazil in 1977, the year before she died. Being her seatmate on a flight between Rio de Janeiro and Salvador da Bahia gave me an opportunity to chat at length with her about my work in medical student education and administration at the University of British Columbia. More and more women were beginning to study medicine then, and I found myself fascinated by this cultural shift. I began to examine the sex-role differences of women and men medical students toward their patients, their educational expectations, their socialization patterns, and their dating practices and marriages. As I shared this with Dr. Mead and our conversation evolved, she made a point of saying to me that I was a feminist. I had never been characterized in this way before, but the moment stuck with me, and it was galvanizing. In 1980, I became Chair of the Pacific Northwest Division of Psychiatrists for ERA, in 1982 I joined the Task Force on Women's Issues of the American Orthopsychiatric Association, and in 1984 I joined the National Organization for Men Against Sexism. Beginning in 1981, I published a few articles on the topic that garnered attention, such as "Sexual Inequality in Medical Care,"[5] "The Professional Woman as Patient: A Review and an Appeal,"[6] and "Women, Not Girls."[7]

All of this was grist for the mill and another dimension of becoming a doctors' doctor. I began to grow as a male psychiatrist, especially in my work with women doctor-patients, and reviewed in earnest what was known in the published literature. As I did for medical students, I wanted to increase my intellectual understanding of the lives of women physicians – their drives and ambitions, challenges in training and practice, sexism in medicine, sexual harassment, economic disparities and intimate relationships. And in my treatment of women doctors, whether as individuals or with their husbands or same-sex partners, I listened carefully, with thoughtfulness and respect. I literally could feel my empathy expand. Here is an example of a female physician and her husband whom I treated in the 1980s:

"Dr. W had had nothing but bad experiences with the male psychiatrists whom she had consulted in the past. I saw her with her husband and she opened the visit with: 'I want to be frank with you. I'm not sure if this is going to work, that is, our seeing a male doctor for our marriage. Quite apart from the fact that our marriage is in trouble and we need help, I'm only here because you are specialized in doctors' marriages and because

Tom said he'd rather see a man, than a woman.' After Dr. W and Mr. G, her husband, told me about their marital worries and problems, I asked Dr. W to tell me a bit more about their previous therapy experiences.

"They first saw a psychiatrist toward the end of Dr. W's internship year. 'I was seven months pregnant, and Tom and I were fighting a lot. Probably because of a combination of factors – we hardly knew each other, we had only met one year earlier, we had money worries, and I was tired and irritable much of the time.' Mr. G added: 'And I couldn't find a steady job, which got me down; I was really worried about the responsibility of becoming a father.' Dr. W continued: 'So we went to see Dr. A, who was recommended by my training director. He was terrible. He cut us off in the middle of our first visit and proceeded to lecture me about women in medicine trying to do it all and driving themselves and others around them nuts. He chastised me for my plans to start a residency and to get a nanny. He also told us that in his clinical experience, most husbands of residents 'fool around' and that I should think seriously about that. Tom almost punched him. Needless to say, we never went back.'

"Dr. W then proceeded to tell me about a more recent experience they had with a male psychiatrist, Dr. N. 'Things started out okay. About the third or fourth visit, Tom and I were talking about a fight we'd had the day before and things got pretty heated in the office. Dr. N turned to me and said: 'You do get quite hostile, don't you? I can understand now why you [turning to Tom] withdraw like you do' I was furious and told him I resented his remark. I didn't want to go back the following week, but decided I would and that I'd bring up the incident for discussion. I told him I felt hurt...and picked on...and singled out. What infuriated me, again, was his response to me, which was so patronizing, so stereotypically psychiatric, something like: 'Accepting the truths about ourselves is one of the hardest facets of psychotherapy. I kept my mouth shut and refused to go back to him.

"Dr. W had had a much earlier negative experience with a male psychiatrist whom she saw when she was a medical student. She had become depressed after she and her boyfriend broke up and her grades began to fall. The psychiatrist insisted she take an antidepressant medication, despite her strong reluctance to do so. 'He just wouldn't listen to me. I told him I wasn't that depressed, that I just needed to talk and be listened to and reassured, that I'd be okay, and get better again. He said we could do both. So I took the pills. He still didn't listen. He just asked about side effects and changed the subject when I tried to speak about my feelings.'"[8]

I responded to Dr. W like this: "I am so sorry that you've had such negative therapy experiences before coming here today. I also appreciate your telling me about them. I understand your mixed feelings about this next attempt at getting help." Turning then to both of them, I continued: "It's absolutely critical that each of you feel valued and respected here or marital therapy won't work. I'm happy to take our visits one at a time if you like, and we'll see how it goes. And please, I'd like each of you to let me know if you feel that I've upset you or got it wrong, or if you feel I've sided with one of you against the other. Anything that doesn't feel right, I want the feedback. I want to discuss it and see if we can get things back on track." They both seemed fine with this and I returned to what their issues were and we went from there. I only needed to see them a few times, as they did well with the basic communication strategies that I'd suggested.

Their love for each other was strong and balanced, as was their commitment to family values.

As I look back on this couple's situation, I'm reminded of how far we've come since then. I hope that contemporary women medical students and physicians never have to experience what Dr. W did, and that the era of patriarchal ascendancy and therapeutic superiority is long past. Regarding her not receiving the psychotherapy she knew she needed and requested as a medical student - and prescribed only medication - I am not so certain.

Converting to Judaism

In the autumn of 1983, I enrolled in a weekly Reform Jewish education class. I did this because my daughter was making her Bat Mitzvah in the fall of 1984, and I wanted to have a better understanding of this landmark coming-of-age experience in a young Jewish woman's life. I was raised Roman Catholic but stopped going to church after graduating from medical school in 1966; indeed, it was during medical school that I began to question many of the Church's tenets. I realized I couldn't reconcile my emerging professional identity as a physician with such conservative and rigid beliefs. When my girlfriend, who was Jewish, and I were married in Los Angeles in 1969, we managed to find a liberal rabbi who was willing to perform our ceremony without my having to convert. This was highly unusual – and still is – and I was grateful for his progressive stance. I referred to myself in those days with the common moniker as a "lapsed Catholic." I could never have converted to Judaism at that time given my interior state of religious futility. I easily accepted the notion of matrilineal heritage, that if we were to have children, they would be Jewish. In fact, I was relieved, as I was in no spiritual condition to provide that kind of guidance in our home.

About six months into my Jewish education class, I began to think about converting. I was in my early-40s and wondered about doing this at my age, although I'm not sure what age had to do with it. The rabbi was pleased with my knowledge – I was a vocal participant in class, I asked tough questions, I argued with intelligence, I embraced Jewish history and philosophy with zest, I wrote good essays (according to him), and to the rabbi's delight, I accepted my fledgling Hebrew with humor and determination. So, I got the green light. In the spring of 1984, after my ritual circumcision and mikvah cleansing bath a few days earlier, at a Friday night service, with my family in attendance, I became Jewish.

Consciously, I became Jewish to offset the alienation of being the only person in our family of four who was an outlier. I quickly realized that I'd acquired two new identities. I was no longer a husband and father, I was a Jewish husband and Jewish father. I reveled in this process, and I call it a process because it didn't happen overnight. I became more relaxed and joyful and intimate in my marriage. As a Jewish parent, I was now able to actively participate in both my daughter's Bat Mitzvah and my son's Bar Mitzvah three years later. I will never forget the indescribable awe and love that I felt standing on the bimah of the synagogue and reciting aloud a Hebrew prayer just before each of my children read from the Torah. It is hard to describe the intensity.

But what about the unconscious and not-so-conscious impact of becoming Jewish -what's that got to do with becoming a doctors' doctor? A friend asked me this once, whether I now was able to "work better" with my Jewish physician patients. I hedged. At first, I told him yes, I can certainly appreciate how certain cultural and religious rules and beliefs of Judaism inform the symptoms and behaviors of psychiatric illness, but that is a rather superficial form of empathy. And then, I said no, that a convert like me can never fully identify with someone who was born and raised in a Jewish home. And that my ability to empathize with that particular physician-patient will be formed by the many issues that transcend religion, as in all therapeutic encounters.

The sense of belonging that I now felt in my family extended much further, into my professional life as a psychiatrist, including my identity as a doctor to other doctors. This includes a sense of affinity, of fitting into the place or role of helping other physicians, with enhanced confidence and purpose. And even though my work has always been secular, there are certain fundamental beliefs in Reform Judaism that have served me well in my quest to help my colleagues. A commitment to social justice, inclusiveness and acceptance of others, progressive ideology and community affiliation are a few of these. The banner is Tikkun Olam, which means "Repairing of the World." It is not a stretch to see how much these principles come into my office, how much they color the doctor-patient relationship, how much they open my mind and heart to the torment, otherness and shame of my patients - and how much they fuel my advocacy on behalf of physicians struggling to survive in our contemporary medical world.

My Clinical Teaching Work

After completing my residency, I worked half time on an in-patient unit of the Vancouver Shaughnessy VA Hospital, one of the University of British Columbia's teaching hospitals. My team consisted of a psychiatry resident and two or more medical students doing their four-week clerkship in psychiatry. I did this for about fifteen years and always enjoyed it. Teaching keeps us up to date, but there was an ancillary benefit for me - I found that getting to know the residents and medical students, albeit limited by time and appropriate boundary constraints, helped me in my practice when I was treating trainees. As the years went on, I could see firsthand that the culture of medical training was changing, that it was not the same as when I trained, both the good and the bad. This is important because even today too many of our medical school professors and clinical supervisors are using an outdated model in their teaching. What is worse and so inappropriate are the ones who admonish their students with statements like: "I don't know what you guys are bellyaching about. When I was a resident, I worked twice as many hours a week and got paid half as much as you do." I've been teaching for over fifty years, and I've yet to meet a medical student or resident who is comforted in any way by this kind of talk.

I have always been careful to pay attention to what hat I'm wearing when I've had a medical student or resident who is struggling at work. One can't refrain from using basic skills that are acquired in training and honed by experience, but it is critical not to slip into treating someone whom you're training. Once again, I have learned so much about the hurdles our students confront as they progress through their training years. Here is an example that I remember well from about five years into my teaching position at Shaughnessy:

I had just finished supervising another of my residents whose patient was getting ECT (electro-convulsive therapy) and came onto the inpatient unit. As I was getting the team assembled to meet in the conference room for rounds, our chief resident - I'll call him Dr. Gladstone - pulled me aside to fill me in about what had happened just that morning. Both my resident - who I'll call Dr. Arthur - and one of my medical students, who I'll call Ms. Wong -had just been told that a patient they had looked after three weeks earlier on one of the medical units had died the day before. He was a 29-year-old man with schizophrenia and diabetes. He was discharged about two weeks earlier and referred back to the clinic where he was receiving care. He had hanged himself. The chief resident said: "They're pretty shook up." I told the charge nurse that rounds would be delayed so I could meet with all of them, which I did.

Here are the highlights. Dr. Arthur had never lost a patient to suicide before. Even though he was no longer the patient's doctor, he was questioning his assessment of the patient and whether he and his supervisor (they had both seen the patient in consultation when Dr. Arthur was on call over a weekend) had missed anything. In fact, the consultation wasn't called because the patient was a problem on the medical unit; the endocrinology team simply wanted guidance on their patient's psychiatric medication while he was in the hospital. He seemed kind of stunned and kept shaking his head in disbelief. Ms. Wong had been doing her internal medicine clerkship and was assigned this patient, so she had come to know him a bit better. "I don't think I did anything wrong. I mainly focused on his diabetes and how that was being treated. What's upsetting me is shock. I just feel terribly sad. He is…was…so young.

Yes, he had schizophrenia, but he seemed sort of okay with it. I didn't ask him questions about his illness but he didn't seem down or discouraged. He said he was getting a lot out of the program he was attending."

After giving each of them a chance to talk and express their thoughts and feelings, I looked at Dr. Gladstone but remained silent. He read my non-verbal communication correctly. He knew this is how teaching units work and that he was next in the order of seniority. He was wonderful. I can't remember his exact words but he turned to Dr. Arthur and Ms. Wong and said something like: "It's a privilege to be with you two. You are both having a normal reaction to this. Suicide happens in psychiatry. When I lost a patient two years ago, what helped me the most was talking about it, over and over and over again. It helped to talk to my supervisor but what was most helpful was talking to my peers." Then he looked at me and said: "So, Dr. Myers, would you be okay excusing them from rounds this morning? It's a beautiful day out. I'd like the three of us to go for a walk and talk a little more. I will oversee their patients when we get back. If there are any concerns that I can't handle, I'll call you at your office. What do you think?" This sounded like a great plan to me.

This is an example of how teaching and the humanistic dimensions of that endeavor has intersected with and informed my clinical work as a psychiatrist looking after physicians as patients. My teaching has also been enriched and strengthened by the many insights I've gained from treating doctors in distress. Bearing witness to their vulnerabilities, their woundedness, their traumas and losses - and having a window – a very special one at that – to their souls has changed me profoundly. When I'm teaching a student who seems kind of wooden or guarded or unduly defensive, I've got hunches as to what might be lurking behind that persona. And without even going there, because that's not my job as a teacher, I can still approach them with level-headedness and respect.

References

1. William M. Sotile and Mary O. Sotile, *The Resilient Physician: Effective Emotional Management for Doctors and Their Medical Organizations* (Chicago: American Medical Association, 2001)

2. Ezra Griffith, *Belonging, Therapeutic Landscapes, and Networks: Implications for Mental Health Practice* (New York: Routledge, 2018)

3. Michael Rowe *Citizenship and Mental Health* (New York: Oxford University Press, 2015)

4. Michael F. Myers, *Why Physicians Die by Suicide: Lessons Learned from Their Families and Others Who Cared* (New York: Michael F Myers/Amazon Publishing, 2017) 32.

5. Michael F. Myers, "Sexual Inequality in Medical Care," *Canadian Medical Association Journal* 124 (1981) 672.

6. Michael F. Myers, "The Professional Woman as Patient: A Review and an Appeal," *Canadian Journal of Psychiatry* 27 (1982) 236-40.

7. Michael F. Myers, "Women, Not Girls," *Canadian Medical Association Journal* 129 (1983) 920-21.

8. Michael F. Myers, *Doctors' Marriages: A Look at The Problems and Their Solutions* (New York: Plenum Medical Book Company, Second Edition, 1994) 76-77

Chapter Three

Beginning to Teach and Write About Treating Doctors

"Every secret of a writer's soul, every experience of his life, every quality of his mind is written large in his works."

Virginia Woolf, *Orlando*. (St. Petersburg: Palmyra Classics, 2017) 180.

I have always been somewhat driven, and I attribute that to my father, my first male role model. He managed to earn his law degree from Osgoode Hall Law School at York University in Toronto during the Great Depression. In addition to attending classes, he worked two part-time jobs cleaning offices to pay for accommodation and food, while scrambling together other bits of money from his father, scholarships, and loans for tuition. But his subsequent career was more than full-time. He ran a busy private practice, managed our family farm after my grandfather died, served many years on Chatham, Ontario's city council and ran twice, unsuccessfully, for provincial member of parliament. Pretty impressive. But as much as I admired and respected him, I didn't want to be like him. His whole life was his work, and typical of male professionals of his era he was the consummate breadwinner, but a distant and absent husband and father. Following in his footsteps a generation later, I was determined to have more balance in my life, including being a functioning husband and engaged father.

Some of my drive has been fueled by my training and practice as a physician. Hard work is part of the job description, the mantle of having Dr. before one's name or MD after it. Doctors feed off each other, and even when we're not competing our self-definition is far too colored by quantitative measures, such as how many hours we work each week or how many patients we see in a day. But I believe that my ambition and pressure for achievement is a result of other things, too. Part of it is curiosity – medicine, and especially psychiatry, has always excited me and given me a hunger for more – and part of it is basic insecurity, because I feel calmer and more confident pursuing scholarly activities.

By the early- to mid-1980s, which bracket the first decade after I completed my training, I knew that I wanted to be doing more than teaching medical students and residents year after year. And I felt the same way about my private practice. But what came next wasn't rooted in boredom or routine - it was just the opposite. I realized that I could weave my ten years of clinical experience into my teaching and work with patients. Two paths opened up at once for me. One was academic and scholarly; I began giving papers at national and international meetings and participating in panels and workshops with like-minded colleagues from afar. The other was governance; I began serving on committees and councils of the Canadian and American Psychiatric Associations. There was much overlap, because I met others who were, like me, with a foot in both camps. This was the beginning of a level of professional development that has enhanced and nurtured my journey as a doctors' doctor. I brought new learning and insights into my daily work with my doctor-patients, and extracted and distilled impressions, emotions and thoughts arising from my therapeutic work with them into my clinical research.

A Young Man Who Taught Me a Lot

This is a true story that has been read and approved by my patient for disclosure.

What follows are the initial paragraphs of a letter written by my patient, DJ, a 24-year-old medical student, to a classmate of his:

"Summer, 1985

Dear Diane [pseudonym],

You may or may not be surprised to learn that I am writing to you from my bed in _____ Hospital. This is an extended care psychiatric unit. I am here because I am no longer able to cope with the loneliness, confusion, despair and fear that have dominated my life since last December. I thought that when our exams ended that my situation would improve. It has not and I am very afraid it will not. I have reached the end of the road. I am at a point where either my life will improve or I will end it.

I am very fortunate in that I have a doctor [Dr. Myers] *who is bending over backwards in an attempt to help me. He is the same psychiatrist that Bill Owens* [pseudonym, another medical school classmate] *dealt with. Dr. Myers is an excellent person, but he is only able to help me in a professional, or if you like, a clinical sense. That is why I decided to write to you.*

Since Christmas, you have been very supportive. I am very grateful for that. You (although you don't realize it) kept me going and were very important to me. I know you are busy enjoying your hard-earned summer vacation but could I ask for your assistance one more time? I would very much appreciate it if you could come to Vancouver and visit me in the hospital. Don't worry about the money: I will gladly pay for the trip. If you could come this weekend, you could stay in my apartment and have the use of my car. If you can't come, please write and let me know that someone cares. I don't have anyone to turn to.

Let me tell you about life here at 'Club Med.' There are twenty patients who supposedly all have the same or similar problems. I find it very difficult to imagine that I have sunk so low as to be compared to these poor people. Two months ago, I was DJ the medical student. Last week I was DJ the summer Research Assistant, learning about recombinant DNA technology. Now am I DJ the loony? If I am, will I ever get better?"

This letter was penned the day after I admitted DJ to the hospital from my office. I had seen him for the first time on an urgent basis ten days before. He was clearly depressed and despairing, explaining to me that he was hopeless and that no one could help. I started him on an antidepressant medication and met with him briefly every day in my office to keep an eye on him and watch for thoughts of suicide. His mood picked up a tiny bit but this was short-lived and spotty. On the day of admission, I had seen him a few hours earlier in my office. He was agitated, sleep-deprived and struggling with looking me in the eye. When pressed, he admitted to a plan to end his life by overdosing on pain killers that he had stockpiled at home. He reluctantly agreed to be admitted to the hospital. He lived alone, and there was no one he could call for a ride; I couldn't trust that he'd make his way there on his own, so I put him in my car and drove him myself. What a harrowing journey! He was exceedingly restless and frightened. He kept wondering aloud if this was all a big mistake and questioned his consenting to be admitted. He was rocking frantically in my front seat, and I prayed for green lights because stopping at any point along the way seemed like an eternity, and I was terrified that he would bolt from the car at any moment. I tried my best to mask my fears by speaking calmly and quietly to him and making reassuring statements that he'd feel safe in the hospital where we could help him with more intensive treatments. When we pulled up to the front entrance of the psychiatry unit, there was absolute quiet in the car, and I was mute with relief that we had made it. I think that DJ's own silence was more about resignation, and capitulating to the wishes of his doctor.

Here is a brief summary of what amounted to a twenty-three-year relationship with DJ. He improved quickly in the hospital with a higher dose of medication, close observation, nursing care, occupational therapy and the psychotherapy program. He was discharged after ten days. Unfortunately, his mood, thinking and behavior deteriorated rapidly over the next few weeks and he needed to come in again. This time I requested a second opinion by a respected colleague of mine who recommended ECT. He eventually felt much better with several treatments and was discharged again. He returned to medical school in the fall, but he was not fully recovered and continued to struggle. At the end of the academic year, it was decided with the Dean's office that he repeat the year. At first, he was embarrassed, but after a few weeks came to accept the wisdom of this decision. He did much better, graduated, and was admitted to a highly competitive residency in another city. He was fine until his final year when he got sick again, but seeing a psychiatrist there and restarting medication were salutary. After he returned to Vancouver in 1996, I continued to follow him until 2008, and with the exception of one brief recurrence he remained well and stable. Tragically, he lost his brother to cancer, but he weathered this terrible loss with equanimity, dignity and expected grief. He has been happily married for years now and is successful in his career, enjoying a national reputation in his branch of medicine as a subspecialized expert.

Lessons Learned

Let's start with DJ's letter to Diane. He captures in simple prose what it's like to be a patient confined to a psychiatric unit. He begins with: "You may or may not be surprised to learn..." - a generous overture to her as he wonders about her state of mind upon reading the letter. If she is surprised, given how much she has been a supportive arm for him over the months, then she might have underestimated how low he was. Or if she isn't surprised, then she's perhaps known for a while that his situation was not improving and this was his fate. Next, he lists the ways he has been feeling for the past six months, all very sad - and concerning. Like most people with entrenched clinical depression, he didn't feel better when his exams were over and the pressure was off. He is now at a crossroads – he either gets better or he will take his own life.

He goes on to describe me as "bending over backwards." As complimentary as this is about my efforts to help, it also speaks to his inner state, that he is a hopeless case and perhaps can't be helped. "Bending over backwards" also implies that I've been going out of my way to help him, and that he hasn't worked along with me or actively participated in the endeavor or been sufficiently grateful. Or maybe even that he doesn't deserve to be assisted. All of these feeling states and thoughts plague the minds of depressed individuals. They are hard on themselves and can't see or accept that they are too ill to meaningfully engage. They don't realize the horrific power of depression and what it does to the mind, spirit and body – how it robs them of core vitality and the ability to connect.

But he also makes a pivotal distinction here between how we professionals are viewed by our patients and how their friends might be. He needs something else, something that a psychiatrist, no matter how well intentioned and heartfelt, cannot give. He needs the help – and dare I say affection or love – of a friend. And therein lies the reason for his overture to Diane.

The next paragraph is heart-wrenching. His loneliness is palpable and stark. Acknowledging how grateful he is to Diane for all she has given in the past, and not wanting to disrupt her summer break, he reaches out one more time. Hat in hand, he offers her money, accommodation and transportation in exchange for a visit in the hospital. This is humility - usually an admirable trait in all of us - but the added twist here is what psychiatric illness and hospitalization does to one's self-esteem and self-regard. He has been diminished and altered by his disease and the requisite hospital treatment, factors that we as mental health caregivers must never forget - or minimize. Visits from friends become visits of the representatives from the outside world, the link to normality, sanity and anticipated return. These encounters are precious.

"If you can't come, please write and let me know that someone cares. I don't have anyone to turn to." These two sentences are a lens into his soul. He is telling Diane that he will understand if she can't visit, a very kind statement coming from a person who, despite his own despair and personal demons, is able to appreciate that the lives of others go on in fulfilling ways. He lets her know that he just needs a response from her and that she cares. He has no one else, and that is subjective and unadorned aloneness.

I thought of DJ's letter about fifteen years later when I interviewed a psychiatrist for a videotape that I produced on physician suicide. She had attempted suicide many years earlier during her residency and was now looking back on that time when she felt so bereft and alone. Her words were: "You feel alienated, that you're outside the world. One of the saddest things about depression is that you look out at the world and people doing normal things and you can't relate to it. You would give anything to be like that. Going to the grocery store…" She too talked about the state of abject aloneness.

In DJ's next paragraph, he rues his old life and what he's lost. He is no longer a medical student, no longer a research assistant — and he queries whether he is now a "loony" like the unfortunate others on the psychiatric unit. What he doesn't know is that his losses are temporary, and that he will regain his health and purpose. Looking around at the other nineteen patients in his unit, reassurances from medical and nursing staff could ring hollow in someone so forlorn. He might even have mused that they too were told the same things years ago by their psychiatrists and other staff — and look where they are today.

My focus on DJ's note in the above paragraphs is to underscore how much I learned about him via this medium. Had he not shown me the note — and given me a copy for his medical record — would I have truly grasped how he was feeling? Would this have come out in my admitting examination, in my daily rounds with him, in the nursing and occupational therapy notes? Would he have even told me? Would I have even asked? In my work with other patients, and in rushing off to supervise my medical students and residents, would I have taken the time to simply sit with him, to be present, to bear witness and not recoil? "Illness is the night-side of life, a more onerous citizenship. Everyone who is born holds dual citizenship, in the kingdom of the well and in the kingdom of the sick." wrote Susan Sontag in *Illness as Metaphor*.[1] Essential reading for any physician who treats other physicians.

But there was another big lesson with treating DJ, as I realized early on that I could not treat him in isolation and with a traditional one-on-one psychiatric model. I interviewed on more than one occasion three of his best friends from medical school, all women, all who cared deeply about him, but who at times grew weary and discouraged. Was he going to get better? Would he become more independent again? Would he get his confidence back? Would he succeed in medical school? Was medicine right for him? I met with his mother and father, both together and alone. They needed information. They needed guidance. They needed hope. I read and kept his mother's letters to me, letters full of emotion, reflections, and gratitude. I spoke with his research advisor. I spoke with two different Deans. I conferred with his psychiatrist where he completed his residency. After he married, I met his wife, and then later consulted his primary care physician following my final visit with him. Yes, it takes a village, so the African proverb goes, but he deserves no less.

National and International Teaching

In April of 1983, I presented a paper at the Wellesley Centers for Women at Wellesley College in Massachusetts, the largest academic institute in the United States devoted to advancing gender equality, social justice and human wellbeing through research, theory and action.[2] The early draft of my paper was titled "The Woman Physician and Her Marriage," a work in progress that grew out of my private practice treating women doctors with troubled marriages. It was a composite of my observations, insights and therapeutic recommendations. There was little research at that time on the marriages of women physicians, in part because we were still in the first decade of more women studying medicine. I also stood out because there were no other male clinicians writing and presenting papers on this subject. This unique status was not lost on me - I felt both excited and scared as hell - but my trepidations abated the moment I was introduced to Dr. Jean Baker Miller.

Dr. Miller, a psychiatrist, psychoanalyst, feminist and writer, was Director of the Stone Center Counselling Service at Wellesley College. I had read her book *Toward a New Psychology of Women* and loved it.[3] Her notions of women and men in relationships were incisive and visionary, and I incorporated many of her insights into my understanding of the marital dynamics of women doctors and their husbands. Meeting her in person was the highlight of my day, including telling her how much of a mentor she was to me. She put me at ease immediately and I was able to deliver my paper, now titled "Overview: The Woman Physician and Her Marriage," with confidence, fluidity and respect. The discussion period with their esteemed faculty and graduate students was challenging and robust, exceeding my expectations. I came away with feedback that was genuinely helpful in revising and improving my original paper, which I presented at the 1983 American Psychiatric Association Annual Meeting, and again a year later at the 1984 Federation of Medical Women of Canada Annual Meeting. The paper was also published in *The American Journal of Psychiatry*.[4]

The most important corollary of this story is how my scholarly work and collaboration with colleagues informs my clinical acumen and therapeutic skill. Sir Isaac Newton's metaphor that we "stand on the shoulders of giants" is a big part of me. I may be alone in my office with a distressed or forlorn couple sitting opposite me, but I don't feel alone - I'm strengthened by the wisdom of peers and those who have taught me so much.

Publishing My First Book

I never thought I would write a book – it seemed wildly ambitious to me, and far above my reach - but two things happened that changed my mind. First, as for many physicians in their early career stage, my success at getting work published in journals - even non-peer-reviewed ones - was fairly dismal. I had no close clinical colleagues who were publishing and no one to critique my work or assist with manuscript guidance. Second, while attending a medical meeting, I happened upon a workshop with the seductive title "Getting Published" - and so I wandered in. That was the game-changer. One of the presenters happened to be a clinician, not an academic researcher, and like me he wanted to write about his clinical experience and the learning that came from that. Though he realized his work did not conventionally fit with top-notch peer-reviewed journals, he started writing books nevertheless.

After the meeting, I let the idea percolate for a while. I had now been in private practice for almost fifteen years and looked after many doctors with troubled marriages. I felt I had something to say – and that there was a need for a book on the topic. I researched the mechanics of finding a publisher, created a prospectus, and started mailing out hard copies. After a few rejections, though not as many as I expected as an unpublished book author, I signed a contract with Plenum Publishing in New York and *Doctors' Marriages: A Look at the Problems and Their Solutions* appeared a year and a half later, in 1988.[5] I was honored – and delighted – when Dr. Carol Nadelson, at that time Professor of Psychiatry at Tufts University School of Medicine, and first female president of the American Psychiatric Association, accepted my invitation to write the Foreword to the book. Here are a few of Carol's sentences:

"Dr. Myers' careful, sensitive presentation of clinical cases from his own practice offers the reader the opportunity to listen "over his shoulder." His contemporary perspective is enriched by his clinical experience and expertise, and his ability to share with us his professional as well as his personal life and thoughts."[6]

A word about writing the book. This was on top of my full-time day job, and I had a year to deliver the finished manuscript to my editor at Plenum, Janice Stern. I was determined that I was not going to let this project encroach on my marital and family time. I was smart enough – and moral enough - to see the duplicity and fraudulence of a psychiatrist writing a book on how to help doctors with their marriages while neglecting his own spouse and children. So, I set my alarm earlier than usual, and in a disciplined manner wrote every day between 5:30 and 6:30 in the morning, five days a week for a year, adding a few more hours when possible on the weekends. And it worked!

But I also found that writing such a clinical book took me to a different level with my patients. I had trouble articulating this, but I was convinced that the rigor and focus of writing made me more expansive and sensitive to my patients. About ten years later, while reading Anne Lamott's epic *Bird by Bird: Some Instructions on Writing and Life*, I did a full stop when reading this paragraph: *"We write to expose the unexposed. If there is one door in the castle you have been told not to go through, you must. Otherwise, you'll just be rearranging furniture in rooms you've already been in. Most human beings are dedicated to keeping that one door shut. But the writer's job is to see what's behind it, to see the bleak unspeakable stuff, and to turn the unspeakable into words — not just any words but if we can, into rhythm and blues."*[7] I was stunned. I realized in this passage why I wrote *Doctors' Marriages*. I had become a conduit, a chronicler of locked-up pain and unhappiness in physicians, and their stories needed to be told. My therapeutic work with doctors in the privacy of my office may have given them personal release and freedom, but my writing paid homage to the complexity and authenticity of their lives. I also wanted the public to see the "rhythm and blues" of working doctors and the broader personal identity that lies behind their healing persona.

Included in my Acknowledgments section is the following:

"This book of course would not be written were it not for the many medical student and physician-patients, and their spouses, who have consulted me over the years. I am thankful to all of them and feel empowered by their faith and trust in me as a therapist. I hope they share my mission in attempting to help others by writing about a subject so dear to almost all doctors. For in essence this is not really 'my' book but 'our' book as a collective of doctors."[8]

I was pleased with the reviews of the book in various publications, but most meaningful to me were the statements of doctor friends, colleagues or strangers who came up to me after lectures: "Your book gave me permission to go and get help… I realized that I'm not the only doctor with problems."

There was at least one doctor who had an extremely negative reaction to the book, and told me so in no uncertain terms. This individual wrote me a letter, which unfortunately has been lost over the years, but the essence of it read like this:

Dear Dr. Myers,

I am a family physician who has always admired your work. I was pleased to purchase a copy of Doctors' Marriages *which I was enjoying until I came upon the chapter on gay and lesbian physician "marriages." I didn't read any further. How could you desecrate a book on married doctors by including relationships that are illegitimate? And wrong. Shame on you. Here's your book back. I'm one reader who doesn't want this book in my home.*

The letter was unsigned and the year was 1989. I've always been aware that physicians are far from monolithic and share a range of values from conservative to progressive, but it was the strength of this physician's disgust that I remember so clearly. The book was based on my clinical experience with a myriad of physician couples, representing the mosaic of doctors practicing medicine in Canada at that time. I reflected upon the many disguised case vignettes in my chapter on same-sex couples, courageous individuals whose relationship strain was in part due to the lack of acceptance by their respective families, society at large, or medical colleagues. Reprinted here is an example, from the social prejudice section of the chapter:

"A few years ago, I was treating a gay medical student, Sam, and his partner of three years, Tom. Their main problem was a sexual one which was rooted in Sam's having been severely sexually assaulted some years earlier while an adolescent. In one session they arrived feeling furious, dejected, and not speaking to each other. They gave an account of a major argument they had had forty-eight hours earlier which included a lot of name-calling, mudslinging, hitting below the belt, and so forth. I was taken aback by all of this because they had been doing very well for several weeks. When I asked about possible precipitants, initially they could not think of anything; they had been out walking the entire day and enjoying each other's company. Then Tom mentioned an incident that occurred as they were nearing their home. A carload of young men pulled up to the curb and started taunting them with suggestive antigay remarks and gestures. One yelled out: 'Hi girls, want some real men?' They didn't persist and quickly drove off, as Sam and Tom tried to ignore them and dismiss the entire experience. But try as they may, they weren't able to forget. The statements of the men in the car upset their equilibrium and provoked their own internal homophobia with resultant upset and retaliatory rage, which they took out on each other. Both ended up feeling emotionally bruised and battered, and completely demoralized about their future together."[9]

In my discussion of this couple, I wrote about social support being fundamental to the growth and stability of coupled people, and that almost all married couples have the acceptance and blessing of their families, friends, acquaintances at work, even neighbors. Not so for gay couples, including Sam and Tom, back in the late 1980s. And this is why I found the tone – unacceptance, judgment, revulsion - of this anonymous physician's letter so upsetting. At first. But then I sprung into gear, and the letter quickly became grist for the mill. It merely redoubled my efforts at doing my best to help gay and lesbian couples in my practice – and to step up my advocacy. And I regifted the book to one of my medical students, who was happy to have it on her bookshelf.

Teaching About Treating Doctors

In 1990, I taught a half-day course - together with a psychiatrist and colleague, the late Dr. Leah Dickstein - at the spring meeting of the American Psychiatric Association called "Treating Medical Students and Physicians." Leah was Associate Dean for Student Affairs at the University of Louisville in Kentucky, and in addition to her administrative duties had treated a number of medical students in need. Combined with my lengthy experience treating physicians in my practice, we created a curriculum that we thought would be of educational value to psychiatrists at the annual scientific meeting. Our objectives were to outline the most common stressful issues for students and physicians, to identify those with a psychiatric illness, to assess and treat them comprehensively with a "biopsychosocial" lens, and to advocate for those who, because of stigma, needed someone to fight for their rights. Our philosophy and guiding principles were that medical students and physicians, while no different than others in their fundamental humanity, do, in fact, require a unique or special approach. If not, they will fall through the cracks and not receive the care they need and deserve.

We were delighted that quite a few psychiatrists and several psychologists and clinical social workers signed up for our course. These were all individuals, usually recent graduates, who were beginning to treat medical students and physicians in their home communities. The APA is the largest attended psychiatric meeting in the world, so our course attracted folks from a number of different countries. Many felt isolated in their work and cherished the idea of meeting counterparts who were struggling with similar challenges when treating doctors and their families, irrespective of their geographical location. The same basic principles apply when treating a suicidal doctor in Nairobi, Kenya or a suicidal doctor in Columbus, Ohio. Taking ethnocultural nuances and stigma into consideration, you don't compromise your high standards - you keep the individual safe, and take charge with empathy and compassion.

This course was reviewed favorably, and we were invited back to teach it again. And again. And again, for twenty years running. We learned from each other and we certainly learned from the evaluations. There were many revisions made to meet educational needs and expectations, especially as circumstances and ideas changed over two decades in the world of medical education and clinical practice. But apart from the pedagogical insights that our graduates took away, the fellowship and collegiality of the yearly event was a valuable byproduct. We always broke up into small working groups over the four hours and they were essential. And intimate. Attendees were free to speak, with confidentiality assured, about disguised details of their challenging patients, about keeping good boundaries when you live in a small town and treat other doctors, about being disparaged by doctor patients who were unhappy with their care, about the sadness of treating doctors with severe and treatment-resistant mood disorders, about losing a physician-patient to suicide. With this course, Leah and I created a safe place, a venue where psychiatrists away from their practices could let their hair down and be candid with colleagues who over the span of a few hours were no longer strangers. Many exchanged phone numbers and emails at the end of the day.

After teaching this course for so many years, I always felt recharged when I returned home to my practice. The trigger to new learning might have been a question posed to me by a student in the course about one of their patients that reminded me of one of my current patients. Either how I answered the question, or the input of others in the group, then rekindled my thoughts about my patient. That I might have overlooked an important element in their care – a blood test, a possible medication side-effect, an earlier resistance in psychotherapy, a query from his wife, a moment of blushing, an averted eye gaze - the list goes on. Any lulls into complacency or boredom – a not uncommon accompaniment to long-term care of a patient – would be offset by my sense of revitalization.

Committee Work on Physician Health

In 1988, I was invited to serve on the Committee on the Impaired Physician of the American Psychiatric Association, a committee that I was involved with for the next two decades. After a few years, we found the name restrictive, focusing only on when illness in physicians affects their work adversely, and it became the Committee on Physician Health, Illness, and Impairment. Our primary charge was to identify, study and research the biological, psychological and sociocultural factors that make doctors ill. Our secondary charge was to make sure that doctors got proper treatment, and the earlier the better, before their symptoms might affect their ability to practice medicine with safety and competence.

I found it exhilarating to come together with colleagues from all over North America, each with an interest in and commitment to the health and wellbeing of physicians. We met face-to-face in Washington, DC each September and had regular conference calls throughout the year. Each spring, a few of us participated in a workshop at the annual meeting of the association. Over the years, we covered such topics as reaching out to the families of doctors with illness, the impact of lawsuits on physicians and their families, diagnosing and treating depression in doctors, "the troubling or troubled resident," substance dependence in physicians, treating physicians with AIDS, ethical transgression of boundaries with patients, and gender considerations in treating women and men physicians. We also generated written documents periodically, and in 1994 produced a videotape initially titled "Physicians Living with Psychiatric Illness."

As I took the lead on producing this short documentary, a few words are in order. Once I put the call out to the medical community of Vancouver that I was making this videotape and wanted to interview both a male and female physician, two physicians came forward almost immediately to meet with me, volunteering to tell their stories. I was simultaneously surprised

and hopeful. Given the stigma in doctors about psychiatric illness, especially in the early 1990s, their commitment to going
public was impressive and laudatory. In fact, it was precisely because of stigma and its damaging effects on physician health that
they cared so deeply. Both knew of physicians who had died by
suicide, and they hoped that by talking about their personal travails they might save at least one physician the pain of untreated
illness, and possibly prevent their demise. The taped interviews
were unscripted, and, once edited, the thirty-minute videotape was released in 1994. After favorable reviews at various
medical meetings, the documentary was renamed "Physicians
Living with Depression" and acquired by American Psychiatric
Association Publishing for marketing and distribution in 1996.[10]

This was an exciting milestone for the Committee on Physician
Health, Illness, and Impairment. We were more than proud of
a product now available all over the world. There was a collective sense that our protracted and years-long advocacy efforts
to educate physicians about the serious and elusive nature of
depression had taken a big leap forward. And it was propelled
by two humble and selfless doctors opening up their hearts.
"Karen," an early career emergency physician, walks the viewer
through what she described as her weeks-long "odyssey," trying
to find a psychiatrist in a new city, all by herself, in the midst of
despondency, guardedness, paralyzing anxiety, shattered self-
esteem and suicidal thinking. Fortunately, a medical intern (a
psychiatric nurse before going to medical school) who worked
in the emergency department with her, saw through her professional mask and reached out to her. She contacted a psychiatrist colleague who saw Karen the following day. "Michael,"

a mid-career academic pediatric neonatologist, was in family counseling with his wife, while dealing with an acting out teenage child. His astute therapist sensed a depressive illness and referred him to his primary care physician for fuller evaluation and specific treatment. He educates the viewer about the life-saving benefits of antidepressant medication and psychotherapy. Their stories are very different, as are they in temperament and career stage, but both are articulate and appeal to a wide range of physician learners.

It is a long time ago now that I interviewed these two fine individuals, but I will never forget an emotional moment with each of them during the videotaping. With Karen, it was when she described calling yet another psychiatrist on her list of names and hearing that he (they were all men) was not available to see a new patient. She would hang up and cry for hours with a massive sense of rejection, fatigue and increasing bleakness. She states that it would take her days to get up the energy and voice to call the next doctor on her list. This happened three or four times. As I listened to her recount this, I felt such anger and shame inside me that my profession was so unresponsive and heartless to a colleague in need. I recall thinking to myself "Fuck - this woman could have killed herself!" My moment with Michael was lighter but equally notable. After he mentioned that he was prescribed an antidepressant by his doctor, I asked him how that was going for him. He replied with a big smile on his face: "Well, these things really work!" I laughed and so did he, and I think my laughter was rooted in working in a branch of medicine that is still a bit of a mystery to people, including fellow physicians.

References

1. Susan Sontag, *Illness as Metaphor.* (New York: Farrar, Straus and Giroux, 1978) 3.

2. https://www.wellesley.edu/academics/centers/wcw

3. Jean Baker Miller, *Toward a New Psychology of Women* (Boston: Beacon Press, 1976)

4. Michael F. Myers, "Overview: The Female Physician and Her Marriage," *The American Journal of Psychiatry* 141 (1984): 1386-91.

5. Michael F. Myers, *Doctors' Marriages: A Look at the Problems and Their Solutions* (New York: Plenum Publishing, 1988)

6. Ibid, ix.

7. Anne Lamott, *Bird by Bird: Some Instructions on Writing and Life* (New York: Pantheon Books,1994) 198.

8. Ibid, xvii.

9. Ibid, 102-03.

10. Michael F. Myers, "Physicians Living with Depression," Committee on Physician Health, Illness, and Impairment, 1994 (Washington, DC: American Psychiatric Association Publishing, 1996) Videotape, 30 min.

Chapter Four

Doctors and AIDS: The First Decade

"...to get AIDS is precisely to be revealed, in the majority of cases so far, as a member of a certain 'risk group', a community of pariahs. The illness flushes out an identity that might have remained hidden from neighbors, job mates, family, and friends."

Susan Sontag, *AIDS and Its Metaphors* (New York: Farrar, Straus and Giroux, 1989) 110.

The 1980s were punctuated with darkness – the beginning of the AIDS pandemic. Nineteen-eighty-one is historically marked as the year that the first recognized case of AIDS appeared in the United States; the first case appeared in Canada a year later. In early 1986, I received a phone call from one of the "ground-zero" doctors at St. Paul's Hospital in Vancouver. Much like Bellevue Hospital and St. Vincent's Hospital in New York City, St. Paul's was the epicenter of HIV/AIDS care in Vancouver. He was worried that his small cohort of physicians working on the front lines was in free fall, that his doctors couldn't keep up the pace, and that something needed to be done to help them.

He wondered about organizing a support group, and whether I might volunteer to lead it - my affirmative response was immediate and unqualified. I knew a few of these doctors personally and was awestruck by their commitment and dedication to their patients, and eager to lend a hand in any way possible to keep them well and able to continue their work. We arranged our first meeting for February 20, 1986.

The idea was for us to come together away from the hospital or clinic setting and meet informally in the evening at one of our homes. There were a number of primary care physicians, a pediatrician, two infectious disease specialists, two oncologists, a neurologist, a dermatologist, a gastroenterologist, a hematologist, a pulmonologist, and a psychiatrist - the range of specialties involved in looking after these patients represented what a multi-system disease AIDS was. The only ground rule was that those attending could not "talk shop," because I did not want these evenings to duplicate or mimic clinical case conferences or rounds, all of which these doctors were doing at the hospital during the day. I also strived to get members not to rely on medical jargon – rather, to use plain English, including emotional language. It was tough. I quickly realized that several of the men (not so much the women) needed the formal, stilted and impersonal code of medicine to distance themselves from the emotionally harrowing doctoring they were doing every day.

Stigma and contagion fears were rampant, and these physicians were truly inspirational and heroic in their daily toil. To understand the magnitude of their work, I want to share details from two papers I presented – one, at the International

AIDS Symposium in 1987, called "Burnout: Who Cares for the Caregiver?"[1] and a follow up at the Annual Scientific Meeting of the Canadian Psychiatric Association in 1988, called "Preventing Burnout: A Group for Doctors Who Treat Patients With AIDS."[2] Three of these primary care physicians had treated sixty to eighty patients with AIDS, the psychiatrist over a hundred, the dermatologist three hundred, and in the AIDS clinic where they all worked, there were a thousand patient visits per month.

I explained to these audiences some of the emerging themes and issues that characterized what the doctors shared in the group format. They gave voice to their feelings – of sorrow, anger, impotence, and, at times, relief – about the deaths of patients they had treated, many of whom were felled by the disease in twelve to eighteen months. They vented their frustrations at the insensitivity, ignorance and prejudice displayed by a number of their doctor colleagues about patients with AIDS - at the time, socially marginalized populations of mostly gay and bisexual men, intravenous drug users, and prostitutes – and how many doctors and their affiliated institutions refused to treat these patients. They talked about their weariness and sadness in counseling patients and their families about this disease. They spoke over and over again about their exasperation and preoccupation at the ever-present need for more funding – for research, for drugs, and for staff to assist them in their mission. They were often anguished and terrified about public news items predicting a projected enormous increase in numbers of patients with AIDS - where would they find other doctors to help them? We discussed how essential it was to try and balance their commitment to sick and dying patients with their personal and family life, and that they would be little help to their patients if they didn't take care of themselves by getting enough rest and nourishment. They were practicing battlefield medicine and they needed protection.

But what helped the most was our coming together, month after month, over the period of the next seven years. A shared fellowship that began with several doctors - and over time grew to include almost twenty physicians with a common mission, baring their souls and feeling free to being exposed and vulnerable - was life-saving, restorative, and morale boosting. As their leader and facilitator – and somewhat at arm's length – I witnessed how they had erected defenses to protect themselves. They had to, for how else could such a small group of doctors maintain their tireless work. I remember clearly one of them explaining why she couldn't go to her patients' funerals anymore. Her reasons were two-fold: she was so busy in her clinic that she couldn't afford the time away, but it was also about not being able to incorporate the interlude of normal grieving into her professional role as a caretaker of her patients. She agonized over this decision because, as she said: "I missed saying goodbye to these young men – and their partners – or parents - guys whom I only knew for a few months or a year maybe, but who trusted me to be their doctor, to treat them, to fight for them. It was all very intimate. And then, they're gone. It rips you apart. But even more heartbreaking, another person is lying in that same bed that they died in, within hours."

Medical Students and Physicians with AIDS

Within a short time, we were beginning to see medical students and physicians with AIDS in Vancouver. And a number of these individuals became my patients, ranging from doctors who had recently tested positive for HIV to physicians with full-blown AIDS. What follows is a short description of a phase of therapy with one of my patients, heavily disguised, even though he signed a release for me to use his situation in my teaching. This is a narrative from a course that I was teaching our residents at the time on supportive psychotherapy with critically-ill patients. Dr. Robert Stillman - not his real name - was a young radiologist who became sick shortly after completing his specialty training.

I have been seeing Robert for almost two years, originally for ARC (AIDS-related Complex), now for AIDS. I have watched him slowly weakening as his T-cell count worsens and he gets infection after infection. Developing Kaposi's sarcoma (a type of cancer) six months ago has been especially difficult for him psychologically because he can no longer deny what is happening to him. Since his last hospitalization, he has been talking to me a lot about dying - his fears, his struggles with spirituality, his anger at having to face death at the age of 32, his sorrow at leaving his parents, partner Joe, and his dog Wolf. He worries of course about how they will be when he's gone.

A recent visit with Robert was particularly significant, and emotional for both of us. He talked to me, I felt, with more closeness than ever before. It was all about sex, but it's not the subject of sex that made me feel so near to Robert. He's talked to me a lot about sex before, both when alone with me and when I've met with Robert and Joe together. No, it was something more this time. He told me how much his body is bothering him, that he can't stand how thin he is now, and how wasted his arms and legs are compared to his trunk, especially his tummy. How he has no muscle tone left and feels so sexually unappealing. And how he is so weak that he can barely walk Wolf around the block. He is frustrated that he is too weak to even attempt to use the weights he has at home. Although Joe is attentive and reassuring, Robert worries that he's a terrible sexual partner for Joe because he just hasn't the interest or the energy for sex that he had as recently as three months ago. The thing I find so sad about what's happening to Robert is what he is having to slowly let go of - his sexuality and all that this has meant to him for so many of his adult years. He doesn't like Joe to see him nude now, and puts on his dressing gown when he walks from the bed to the bathroom.

What I wanted to illustrate to my residents with the story of Robert is the ubiquity of loss when treating patients with AIDS, captured so movingly as Robert talks about grieving his relationship with his parents, Joe, and Wolf. And he expands on what AIDS has done to his physical appearance and rigor - his body image is decimated, his sexual drive has waned, and there's a loss of physical intimacy, touch and connection. He is ashamed of his body and has lost the freedom of nakedness with Joe. There is an evolving retreat into aloneness and distance.

My teaching with these young doctors also includes my story, my role in all of this. How essential it is to be present with your patient, to listen with care, to be silent (mostly), and above all, to create and preserve a safe place for your patient to speak freely and with rawness. This also means that as a therapist you suspend, or at least moderate, what you're feeling inside - the melancholy, the unfairness of it all, the rage and existential madness of the disease in someone so young.

Here is another disguised story of one of my patients. He was not at all typical of the doctors I was treating, but his narrative was not unusual among the men in general who developed AIDS during the early decades.

Dr. Green, a 35-year-old single pathologist, was referred to me by his primary care doctor in the fall of 1990. His doctor attended the prevent burnout group that I've discussed above. The reason for referral was Dr. Green's refusal to accept any anti-retroviral drug treatment for his being HIV positive. In my first visit with Dr. Green, his opening words were: "I'm sure that my doctor told you that I'm HIV positive and that I'm refusing all preventive treatment for AIDS. I'm here to say that he's right. So that's a discussion that you and I do not need to have. But I'm okay seeing you because my mood is down and I think I'm depressed." He was correct, he was clinically depressed, so I prescribed an antidepressant for him which he willingly took and he felt and functioned a lot better. My hope was that, as his mood improved and his outlook became brighter and more life affirming, he would consent to anti-AIDS treatment. I was wrong. He became even more fixed in his resistance. What follows are a selection of his verbatim quotes from my notes.

"I'm looking forward to dying of AIDS. Well not the process so much because I don't like pain or the idea of having trouble breathing — but I'll reevaluate my stance on that when I get to that stage. What I mean is that I deserve to die. I'm one sick homosexual who got himself into this mess by my actions and so I must accept the consequences and pay the price of my sinful behavior. I've been struggling with these urges since

I was a boy. But I never gave in to them because I had my faith — I was raised Christian Baptist, very conservative — and although I no longer attend church, I remain certain in my beliefs that homosexuality is wrong, egoistic and warrants damnation. Now that my mood is normal again and I'm functioning better at work, I can at least do more of God's work practicing medicine until my body gives out. I've always considered medicine a calling and I'm grateful to God for whatever time he'll grant me before he calls me to him."

This short segment illustrates how formal he was with me. His language never softened or became less stiff. Once, while trying to learn more about his upbringing, I used the word gay in a question, something like: "What were these gay feelings like when you became a teenager?" He was sharp with me and responded with: "Please don't use that socially permissive word 'gay' — there is nothing acceptable about homosexuality — it is wrong and the work of the devil." In fact, this example was indicative of how I had to tread carefully with him, and his primary care doctor found this to be the case as well. My visits with him were largely supportive of how he was doing at work and monitoring his medication. I was able to determine though that he was not delusional, his reality testing was in place, there was no evidence of cognitive impairment, he was mentally competent, and his capacity to make treatment decisions was intact. In other words, he was of sound mind, he was not psychotic, nor was there any clinical evidence that the virus was affecting his brain functioning. He was safe to be practicing medicine.

I would conclude that I struck out in helping this doctor accept himself in a more integrated and less fragmented manner. It is always hard as a physician when you're thwarted in wanting to help someone. You must lower your expectations and try to simply meet the patient on their own ground. And that is what I did. But I clearly remember how I felt about him – he was desolate and forlorn, especially in his isolation and living alone with his shameful feelings. I only saw Dr. Green for a total of six sessions, as our work together ceased when he made the decision to leave Vancouver and move to another part of the country. About eighteen months after his last visit with me, I read his obituary in a medical journal.

This clinical account took place almost thirty years ago. Certainly, the face of AIDS has changed over the years, as has society's understanding of homosexuality, including a much more accepting house of medicine. If Dr. Green had become HIV positive today, I hope that he would not feel so sinful, or be so self-flagellating and in need of punishment by death. Even though homosexuality was first removed as a diagnosis from the American Psychiatric Association's *Diagnostic and Statistical Manual of Mental Disorders* in 1973, it was not fully re-classified until 1986 – a context which partly explains Dr. Green's painful mental state. And there are certainly many more social supports for individuals who have been raised in religiously conservative homes today than there were then.

As with many physicians who treated HIV patients in these early years, I attended far more funerals than one normally expects to. The story below is also from my teaching notes of that time. It is about the stigma attached to seeing a psychiatrist, and how we psychiatrists have to be ever careful about the covenant of our work with patients and breaches of confidentiality.

Last fall, I attended the funeral of one of my patients who died of AIDS. I'll call him Dan. At the end of the service, his family waited at the back of the church to receive the mourners as we made our way down the aisle. I looked ahead and noticed that Dan's mother was in the middle with his sister on her right and his life-partner Bill on her left. Because I had already met Dan's sister and Bill before in my office, they were aware that I was his psychiatrist. But I didn't know whether his mother knew or not that her son was seeing a psychiatrist. So, I just shook her hand and said: "Hello, Mrs. X, I'm sorry for your loss." To which she said: "And who are you?" I replied with: "My name is Michael Myers." To which she replied with a jolt: "Were you one of Dan's doctors?" I gasped and stuttered "Yes." With that she shook my hand vigorously, pulled me closer to her, looked me straight in the eye, and whispered so the stranger on my left and on my right couldn't hear: "I know which doctor you are ... Dan was very fond of you ... you helped him a lot ... you know AIDS is not an easy disease to have, it gets at your self-respect ... there is just so much misunderstanding out there." I thanked her, told her what a fine man her son was - he truly was, a real prince of a man - and wished her well. As I walked away from the church to my car, I was acutely aware of how humbled I felt in the presence of this wise, gracious and loving woman.

Dr. Peter

Dr. Peter Jepson-Young was a Canadian physician who died of AIDS in 1992. He became a household name when he made the courageous decision in September of 1990 to go public with his disease.[3] His goal was to put a human face to this tragedy and to educate Canadians about HIV infection, to correct misperceptions, and to eliminate much of the antipathy and fear that surrounded it. The fact that he himself was a physician not only increased the appeal and credibility of his messages, but also drove home the notion that doctors are human too, and that we too can be gay and acquire the virus just like anyone else. In 1990, when I first watched a segment of his series called "The Dr. Peter Diaries" on the CBC evening news, disclosing to the Canadian public that he was a physician with AIDS, I was deeply moved. Through a physician colleague at work who was a classmate of his in medical school and who reached out to him, we invited him to give a grand rounds at our teaching hospital.

On the day of the rounds, faculty, residents, medical students, nurses and other health professionals were all assembled as Dr. Peter began making his way into the auditorium, a handsome man in his early thirties, using a white cane. He had just become blind from CMV (cytomegalovirus) retinitis and he was no longer able to practice clinical medicine. His talk was elegant in both substance and human dignity.

Peter and I eventually partnered together at UBC, and given my position as director of medical student education in psychiatry, I was able to slot him into many venues to speak to medical students. Our usual arrangement was for each of us to be seated at the front of the lecture hall, where we would open with a casually structured interview, and then take questions from the audience of students. In all my years of teaching I have never seen students so focused and engaged. They lined up after the lecture to introduce themselves, to shake his hand, and to salute his work on national television. Peter once said to me: "You know Mike, it's kind of weird but there is a bit of a silver lining to this disease – AIDS and being blind. Before I lost my vision, I couldn't find a locum job because I had AIDS and no doctors' office would have me. But now at least I can use my medical training as an educator." I had to agree. He often moved me to tears, but because he couldn't see my moist eyes, I didn't have to worry about derailing him.

It was Peter's idea – which I jumped at – to produce a videotape. I arranged funding and in October of 1990 we made "Physicians With AIDS: An Interview With Peter." In this interview, Peter talked about many subjects: his decision to go public as an openly gay doctor; getting pneumonia; surviving cardiac arrest; living with blindness; the impact of his illness on his family; becoming depressed and seeking help; his ideas about euthanasia and his comfort in possessing a lethal dose of barbiturates should he need it; and his hope.

I showed this tape at the International Conference on Physician Health, and the Canadian Psychiatric Association Annual Meeting, both in 1991, and at the American Psychiatric Association Annual Meeting the following year. Peter and I were both pleased with the reviews, especially one published in 1992:

"In the interview, Peter is revealed as an articulate, sensitive person fully capable of and comfortable with describing the barrage of experiences and suffering that an AIDS patient endures. The interview is sensitive but probing and typifies the kind of dialogue that extracts and illuminates a patient's personal experiences. It provides an outstanding model at

a time when structured psychiatric interviewing is gaining increasing prominence as a modality in itself. The viewer is emotionally captured by Peter's descriptions of the course of his illness, such as the time during his hospitalization for pneumonia when his oxygen tank ran out of oxygen while he was on the hospital elevator. We appreciate Peter's sensitive insight when he describes AIDS as a "disease of barriers" and when he recounts his reactions to everyone's reluctance to touch him during his hospitalization."[4]

Six weeks before Peter died in November of 1992, at the age of 35, we taped Part II. This was a challenging time for him, in that he was quite weak, but he remained unwavering in his commitment to teaching. Over the many months since October of 1990, we had discussed recording a follow-up interview, but actually doing it remained rather abstract. It was Peter who called me in late September and told me he was ready. I hadn't seen him in a few months, and when I picked him up at his home to drive to the studio, I quickly realized how compromised he was. He was extremely short of breath and required oxygen and physical support. He had many Kaposi sarcoma lesions on his face, and I was happy to help him with his makeup - he also let me comb his hair and fix his tie. He didn't want to be filmed using his nasal cannula - "I don't want to look like I'm dying," he quipped - so we did short segments, he'd take an oxygen break, and we'd resume. It took time, and he was deeply apologetic to everyone, but no one was in a hurry. We were all grateful to simply spend time with this remarkable man. His valor and decorum were palpable, and his sense of humor eased the gravity of the moment.

In this interview, Peter discusses candidly with me how his illness has worsened since our first taping - his decision to forego further experimental treatments, his preparedness to die, putting his affairs in order, and saying goodbye to his parents, his sister, her children, his partner Andy and, most evocatively, his seeing eye dog Harvey. The final scene captures my thanking him for the gift of the interview. He extends his hand to me as he says: "Maybe we'll do it again in two years" and I reply: "I hope so, I hope so."

I made the rounds with this production in 1991 and 1992 at the same three annual meetings mentioned above. I was delighted to have Dr. Bertram Schaffner accept my invitation to be the discussant when the videotape was shown at the American Psychiatric Association meeting two years later in May of 1994 in Philadelphia. Dr. Schaffner was a highly respected psychiatrist and psychoanalyst in New York and, most importantly, one of the pioneering psychiatrists to come out as gay in America.[5] Lauded as a kind-hearted gentleman, he was especially eloquent in his posthumous tribute to Peter. As he read from his prepared notes, his composure flew out the window, so fitting of the task at hand. It was a genuinely memorable moment, and my heart was filled with pride and community as I scanned the audience.

Over the years, I have mailed off requested copies of these videotapes to countries throughout Europe and South America, and to Japan, Taiwan, New Zealand and Australia, and while doing this I've imagined how pleased Peter would be that his work has lived on after his death. His legacy has also been enshrined with the Dr. Peter AIDS Foundation in Vancouver, which Peter established just before he died. I was privileged to serve on its Board of Directors several years later.[6]

A Moment in Therapy with a Physician Living with Two Illnesses

Stigma, already so heightened in physicians, was even higher in the doctors I looked after with HIV disease in those early years. It didn't seem to matter whether my patient was gay or bisexual, coupled or single – all felt deeply ashamed and guilty about acquiring the virus. I remember one of my doctor-patients saying: "I think I'm more embarrassed about having bipolar illness than having HIV-disease." When I asked him to elaborate, he responded with: "Well, I'm openly gay and I imagine people are just going to assume I'm positive, so they won't judge me if I were to tell them. But they don't know I'm bipolar and if they did, I think they'd look at me weirdly, as if I'm defective in a way, not to be trusted, like I might go crazy or something like that." This statement became the springboard for much of our psychotherapy together. He gradually came to understand that it was he who was judging himself about his mood disorder, because even though he clearly understood the biology of bipolar illness, he continued to struggle with it. His words were like this: "A biological cause of my mood swings is a cop-out. I'm not supposed to blame myself for a thing I have no control over. It runs in my family, I know that. But I still blame myself anyway. I smoked a lot of weed in college, I just squeaked into medical school. I goofed off a lot. I stopped going to synagogue. This makes more sense to me than fucked up genes." I posed a question to him: "So, becoming bipolar is about punishment?" He paused, smiled slightly, and sat quietly for a few seconds.

"I think it's about control, I'm grasping for control over these two monsters taking over my life" was his insightful response.

AIDS and the Doctor's Family

"Couples who are experiencing marital distress because the man has contracted the human immunodeficiency virus (HIV) present one of the greatest challenges to marital therapists today."

This is the first sentence of a paper that I published in 1991.[7] As one of the few psychiatrists trained in and practicing couples' therapy, I wanted to produce an article that would be helpful to therapists of many disciplines who were treating these complicated couples. I wrote about the psychological struggles for the men, their wives, their children, the marital symptoms to watch for, the goals and types of treatment – and most important, the so-called countertransference issues, the feelings and attitudes that arise in therapists themselves: the upsetting emotions, the threat to one's professional equilibrium, family values and personal ethics. As the 1990s wore on, and in my position as the director of the Marital Therapy Clinic at St. Paul's Hospital, we were now witnessing how the face of AIDS was evolving. We were treating many intravenous drug users and their opposite-sex, same-sex or transgendered partners. We were treating lesbian couples who had become infected from previous heterosexual experiences or drug usage. Many were medically ill, in addition to having AIDS, and many also had one or more other psychiatric illnesses like schizophrenia, bipolar illness or post-traumatic stress disorder. A great number were also socially disadvantaged. Several of our patients who were homeless had fallen in love with each other either on the streets or in shelters. We found that paying attention to the intimacy struggles of these very ill men and women – and their partners – picked up their spirits, gave them immeasurable pleasure, and prolonged their lives. The work was challenging but always gratifying, and the medical students and residents who trained with me were grateful for the experience.

Couples' therapy with HIV-positive doctors was also part of my private practice. Here is one example, a snippet from my first visit with a doctor's wife, herself a physician. We didn't do couples therapy, though it was her marriage that precipitated her individual therapy with me.

Dr. Enid Tade, a 46-year-old ophthalmologist, came to see me shortly after her husband Dr. Mark Ash was diagnosed with AIDS. "I'm still in shock – and it's been a month, a month since my world blew up. What I thought was a perfect world is disintegrating around me." Dr. Tade stopped speaking, became teary-eyed, then began to sob – uncontrollably. I sat quietly, passing her Kleenex tissues, one after another. But her crying intensified, her chest was heaving violently, and she got panicky. I helped her with deep breathing exercises. She regained control. And she whispered "Thank you."

"Mark is bisexual and that's how he got the virus. I had no idea. I never suspected this, never in my wildest dreams. There were no signs, none that I could see, anyway. In fact, to Mark's credit, when I said to him: 'Am I just blind, or stupid, or on another planet, or in denial, or what?,' he told me 'No, you're none of that, I've been a fox, I was determined that you'd never find out.'

"But I can't process this. I thought our marriage was fine. Well, as fine as any marriage after twenty years, two kids, and two busy careers. I guess I was wrong. But Mark says he's been happy too – except for this 'thing' that's been with him all his life, his attraction to guys.

"Anyway, that's enough about that bit for today. I can return to this later. There's more I want to tell you.

"Problem #2 – now, I'm sounding like a doctor, aren't I? The list-maker. But bear with me. I don't want to start weeping again. Problem #2 is my kids. Brad is 18 and Jessica is 14. We haven't told them anything. All they know is that their dad was terribly sick, and it was pneumonia. But Mark and I both agree, they need to be told. But what? And when? Brad's graduating in a few weeks and he doesn't need this kind of stress. He already struggles with school. And Jessica – well, she's 14, what can I say?

"Problem #3 – me. I'm waiting for my HIV test results. For some strange reason, I'm not worried. We are sexually active – I mean we were sexually active – but not that often. I haven't even let my mind go there… that I could be infected too.

"Problem #4 – Mark's practice. He's an academic, a research hematologist. He only sees patients for clinical trials. He doesn't do any procedures – so he's not at risk for harming his patients. But how long can he keep working?

"Problem #5 – we're living with such a big secret – and a dark one, at that. I'm doing damage control. This is our life. I don't want people judging us – both Mark and me. But how do we keep the lid on this? I told my sister, she's my best friend, we're twins. Mark is okay with that. He loves Elaine. He trusts her. But he hasn't told anyone yet, none of his family, or his best friend.

"Problem #6 – and this is the hardest. Mark is going to die. I love him. The kids love him. I'm not ready to be a widow, that's for older women. But I'll do it. I'm a survivor. But when I think of Mark, I get so angry, so sad. This isn't fair. He's such a great doctor, a wonderful husband, a terrific father, and..."

Here is a summary of our work together. The good news, which was a godsend and lessened Dr. Tade's worry list more than she realized, was that she was antibody negative - that is, not infected with HIV. Dr. Ash was greatly relieved by this knowledge as well. But she needed to talk about and tackle her husband's secret life and all of the mixed feelings surrounding that. She was protective and defensive of him. She had a younger brother who was gay, and they were very close, a relationship that was enhanced when their father disowned him and she hovered like a mother hen. Dr. Tade could see the parallels there, but she needed to allow herself to give voice to the feelings of betrayal and violation that anyone feels when a spouse "cheats." And the rage at him – and incredulity - for putting her at risk of getting infected. My job was to help her understand that you can have a confusing cauldron of emotions about someone you love who falls from grace.

Another dynamic that we tackled was her self-esteem. Being a physician and having a gay brother, Dr. Tade certainly knew that homosexuality and bisexuality are not conscious and deliberate sexual or lifestyle choices. But that knowledge did not help her with her obsessive thinking about her role in Dr. Ash's extramarital behavior. She blamed herself for many things that she thought might have driven her husband away from her: that she worked late, was occasionally irritable in the evenings, that she had put on a few pounds, that she was peri-menopausal, less interested in sex, didn't complement him enough. The list went on and on. Eventually, she was able to be less harsh and more forgiving of herself, and to accept that she effectively had no control over her husband's urges and that he alone was responsible for his actions. For a while, she harbored a belief that if her husband had sought psychotherapy for his bisexuality when he was a young man, he might have been able to let it go and become totally straight. She gradually realized that her thinking had a magical quality to it and that sexual orientation is not that simple.

I had one visit with Dr. Tade's children. Both she and her husband requested the appointment and I was pleased to meet with them. That's when I met Dr. Ash, as both he and Dr. Tade brought them into my office. Brad and Jessica, at this point, had known about their dad's situation for several weeks. I was struck by their maturity and poise, and I was also pleased to see what a close relationship they had with each other. Having had scores of visits with children of doctors over the years who are in the midst of divorcing, they were a refreshing contrast. There was a sense of solidarity in these two siblings, that they were there for each other then, and would be as their dad's health worsened and after he died. They pulled no punches. They both talked spiritedly about the anger they felt toward both their dad and their mom, and with less abstraction and intellectualizing than most adolescents. But this gave way to softer feelings, of unhappiness and tenderness, and family alignment with the secrecy surrounding AIDS. I knew this was a loving family, and that they would all pull together in the months ahead.

Dr. Tade had a great sense of compassion for her husband. She was wistful and regretful that he never felt safe enough to talk about his same-sex feelings with her, that he was alone with such "dark and shameful longings" - his language for this. But she was frank too, as in this remark: "If Mark had confided in me, I've got to be honest, I think I'd have freaked out – at least at first – but I think I would have understood. And not judged him like my dad did to my brother. I would have been open, I think, to living with this, as long as he didn't act on it. No way I could handle that, I've heard of wives who do, who have an open marriage, that's not me, I'm clear about that."

As Dr. Ash's condition worsened he needed to retire from his job. He focused on his hobbies at home and began to tidy up loose ends. Dr. Tade took a leave of absence from her work, and was an ever-ready companion to her husband. They enjoyed taking short getaways to see friends and family and sharing weekends at their favorite haunts. She frequently mentioned in visits with me that they had never had such fun, such laughter, such closeness in all their years together. "There aren't any barriers anymore, we don't hold anything back, every moment together is a gift." Dr. Ash was in hospice care for the final two weeks of his life, and Dr. Tade and the children were with him when he died.

Conclusion

In this chapter I've painted the landscape for doctors in the early years of AIDS, whether they were those treating patients with the disease or afflicted themselves. So much has changed in the years since. AIDS remains a serious disorder, but it is now considered to be a chronic illness, no longer a death sentence. Education about the virus and its transmission has reduced the rate of new infections in most men and women, including physicians themselves, and broader knowledge has lessened contagion fears and much of the stigma. Advances in treatment have brightened the prognosis and engendered hope.

References

1. Michael F. Myers, "Burnout: Who Cares for the Caregiver?" Paper presented at the International AIDS Symposium (Vancouver, British Columbia, November 2, 1987)

2. Michael F. Myers, "Preventing Burnout: A Group for Doctors Who Treat Patients with AIDS." Paper presented at the Canadian Psychiatric Association (Halifax, Nova Scotia, September 29, 1988)

3. "Dr. Peter Diaries: AIDS Then & Now" (Vancouver: CBC/Radio Canada, 2018) https://www.cbc.ca/bc/features/drpeter/

4. Ian Alger, "Loss and grief in AIDS and Physicians with AIDS," *Psychiatric Services* 43(9) (1992): 872-73.

5. Jeffrey Langham, "Remembering Gay Pioneer Bertram Schaffner" (Los Angeles: USC Shoah Foundation, 2016) https://sfi.usc.edu/blog/jeffrey-langham/remembering-gay-pioneer-bertram-schaffner

6. Dr. Peter AIDS Foundation (Vancouver, British Columbia) https://www.drpeter.org/

7. Michael F. Myers, "Marital therapy with HIV-infected men and their wives," *Psychiatric Annals* 21(8) (1991): 466-70.

Chapter Five

The Middle Years: Treating, Teaching and Traveling

"When people ask me why I still have hope and energy after all these years, I always say: Because I travel. For more than four decades, I've spent at least half my time on the road."

Gloria Steinem, *My Life on the Road* (New York: Random House, 2015) xvii.

In this chapter, I will highlight some of the events, challenges and opportunities of the middle years of my career - roughly mid-1990s until mid-2000s - and how they influenced my becoming a doctors' doctor. Although I had become a subspecialist in physician health, and was generally known as someone who looks after other physicians, I've always preferred to use the term becoming in its present continuous tense, to express the evolution of my professional life as a dynamic ongoing process of learning in the profession of medicine.

The following true story has been read, slightly altered, and approved by my patient for disclosure.

Jane (a pseudonym) was a 28-year-old senior resident in Cardiology who came to see me for problems in her relationship. She was accompanied by her partner of two years Bruce (a pseudonym) who was an attorney in his early years of practice. They were referred for couples' therapy because they were constantly arguing and fighting, frustrated that their communication with each other wasn't working. Jane was also feeling stressed and burned-out with her residency and upset about recently failing an in-training exam. And in the background was another big stress, the failing health of her beloved grandmother, and her eventual death.

After the first meeting, when I saw them together, my plan was to have an individual visit with each of them alone, then embark on a series of further joint meetings with the two of them together. But tensions escalated and Bruce moved out of their shared apartment about three weeks after our first meeting. They did have sporadic contact, but it was not good. They never returned together for couples' work. It was the abruptness of the breakup that was so devastating for Jane. She crashed (I mean that almost literally) into a suicidal depression. I then became her individual therapist for several years, until the spring of 2008.

Jane's entire being was assaulted by her symptoms. Her mood plummeted ("I've crashed from the moon to the earth"). She was deeply sad and despondent. Her sleep was erratic, broken and fitful. Like many doctors trying to fight off psychiatric illness, she could cope at work in the early weeks, but would collapse as soon as she got home. She spent much of her time in bed. She was overcome with uncontrolled bouts of crying emblematic of her profound grief. Her appetite ended and she lost fifteen pounds over the next few weeks. When she did eat, she retched. She was isolating from her friends and family, she had little energy for anything but work, and she began to lose her ability to concentrate and remember things.

In the early weeks, Jane was obsessed with the relationship and was unable to get it out of her mind. Her statement: "He's amputated me — and tossed me into the garbage" speaks volumes about her sense of self. The unraveling of the relationship was a mystery to her, and she had no opportunity to sort this out with Bruce or to find any semblance of "closure." As with many professional women in situations like these, she questioned her judgment: "How could I have been so wrong?" She had dream-like states that were otherworldly and confusing. Her sleep was punctuated by nightmares with themes full of imagery of aloneness, bleakness and dying. Although she had no actual thoughts of suicide early on, she did have death wishes for relief from her psychic pain and anticipated peace in the afterlife. Her self-esteem was demolished; she often referred to herself as pathetic, useless and whiney. And as if all of this was not enough, she had a number of physical symptoms as well – migraines, unexplained dizziness, numbness and tingling of her fingers and toes, and assorted muscular aches and pains.

Antidepressant medications didn't work for Jane and, if anything, drugs made her feel worse. Electroconvulsive treatment was recommended by two different colleagues of mine, but she was not interested. I met with her weekly for psychotherapy — and for periods, twice weekly — to keep a close eye on her and provide support and guidance. Her family members were worried that her depression was so entrenched and protracted. I met with her mother a couple of times, her brother twice, and once with the whole family. These visits seemed helpful for everyone, and meant a great deal to Jane, insofar as I could perhaps explain things to her beleaguered family that she couldn't. And that if she did die of "all of this" I would be there to console them.

Let me explain what it was like for me, being Jane's psychiatrist. In a workshop that my colleague and co-author Dr. Glen Gabbard and I did together, at a meeting of the American Psychiatric Association on critical issues in the treatment of the suicidal physician, he used the term "Our patients are us." How can we not identify — or overidentify — when it often feels that treating doctors is like looking in a mirror? We see so many of our own conflicts and fears, and that can be terrifying, an emotion I felt on many occasions while treating Jane. She was only a couple of years older than my daughter, and there were parallels.

I also worried about blurring boundaries, so common when we treat physicians. I was especially cognizant of this when the therapist's "real life" dislodges the frame, the predictable certainty of appointment dates and times. This happened when I was President of the Canadian Psychiatric Association. I was away from Vancouver for much of that year and had to cancel and rebook a number of appointments with Jane. We also had telephonic sessions from afar. She never expressed any anger at me for being away. Given the middle-stage of my career when I first began treating Jane, I was quite seasoned and used to treating doctors. But I struggled with diagnostic uncertainty – my reflections ran the gamut from underdiagnosing to over-diagnosing her. She was not progressing according to plan and this frustrated me and made me feel inadequate. My professional confidence took a big hit. Apart from the psychopharmacology and other physician consults that I found helpful, I am indebted to my two office mates, first-rate psychiatrists, who buttressed me over months and years. And I also had two colleagues from afar who gave me sage advice, both skilled and experienced psychodynamically-trained psychotherapists.

During the course of my treatment with Jane, I reviewed the published literature on countertransference (the therapist's re-action) when treating patients with melancholia, and partici-pated in a workshop on the subject at the Canadian Psychiatric Association Annual Meeting. The process helped me understand Jane's anger at the illness of depression, her periodic denial of illness, and her mixed feelings about treatment. I grew calmer with her frustration that she was not getting better faster, her reluctance to take medication, her fear of this illness coming back and the curse of her genes. Reading also helped me to be empathic when she didn't stick to the treatment and she resisted my recommendation for her to do "mood charting." I came to be more understanding of my need to be in control, to be the care-taker, to be wise and knowledgeable, and to be calm when Jane didn't seem to be getting better. Most critically, I had been blind to subtleties in her improvement, so-called "baby steps," because of my zeal and overdetermined expectations as a physician, and her need - and my need for her - to regain her resilience and work performance. I went through periods of obsession with therapeutic drugs and a drive to find the "magic bullet," only to realize that I needed to step back and see the broader picture of what we were doing in treatment.

Jane frightened me with her suicidal despair. From a note she wrote to me in 2003: "It becomes clearer every day, that the stuff I do, working, hanging out with people, even 'fun' things are pointless, meaningless distractions from reality. The reality of knowing that I don't have a purpose here. What is all of this for, everything we work for? Death can't be worse than this. It's getting harder all the time and it astounds me because each day I can't believe that I can actually feel worse than I already do. I can't stop crying. It tears my guts out. I realize that I will not survive this. Yesterday I ran a scalpel slowly across my neck, not touching my skin, just to imagine it, but…"

On many occasions she corrected me that she was not actively suicidal, she just wished for death and peace. I recall vividly one time she verbalized almost these exact words, which I'm paraphrasing here: "You don't need to worry about me killing myself, Dr. Myers. My thinking and energy are so bad that I couldn't do it properly anyway. And you've already made it clear that you're not into mercy killing." In one note, she wrote: "I've been reading Derek Humphry's *Final Exit* – oh, how it speaks to me – I feel old – I'm ready to leave. I also visited online the Church of Euthanasia – I agree with their message, save the planet, kill yourself."

In one session, on a page of paper, she wrote: "I really, really want to die. Just to make it stop. And I'm alone, I've worn everyone out on this. I wonder what other people are doing while I sit contemplating suicide. I can't describe this restless loneliness, the pain I feel from the lack of close physical contact with anyone. This sounds so pathetic. The only living being I've been able to do this with in the past two years is Belle (pseudonym), my horse. When it's dark, I go and feed her. While she's eating, I lean my body against her and lay my head on her side. And I hug her and talk to her and tell her I love her, and I cry. Her warmth and her gentleness are comforting. I wonder if that's what I'm missing here. Just to be held for a while so I can bawl my eyes out."

As I listened to Jane read this passage, I became tearful. She noticed and there was a brief reversal of roles. She passed me the box of Kleenex near her and said: "What's making you cry?" I stuttered: "This is so sad." She nodded in agreement and began to cry. I passed the Kleenex back to her, and, with that, we both started to laugh. It was a moment of intimate connection and empathy about year three of our therapeutic work together. I came away from that session with an almost mystical respect for how immense her existential suffering and isolation was. Instead of trying to make it go away by fixing it (like we want to do as doctors) I simply gave myself permission to be fully present and authentic.

In the years leading up to 2008, Jane slowly improved, and we had less frequent sessions as her medical work became more demanding. Her physical symptoms abated but her depressive and anxious thoughts lingered. She met someone new, and although Jane was wary, their relationship advanced. They lived together for a year or so and then got married. I had three visits with her in 2007, and a final visit in May of 2008, as I was leaving Vancouver and moving to New York City. She brought in a card and a gift that still has a prominent place in my Brooklyn office. I'll close with a few sentences she wrote. The theme is universal, words of a grateful patient, familiar to all of us. But the bigger picture is a definition of psychotherapy and what we bring to that enterprise that we treasure so much:

"There just aren't words to begin to express my appreciation for what you have given me over these many years. My life would have been different had I not had this safe place to come so often. You have a rare and special gift in what you do – that goes without saying. But it was your kindness, generosity, compassion, your humanity, that has filled an empty place in my heart. Thank you. I will miss you very much. With deepest respect, warmth and gratitude, Jane."

Jane and I kept in touch by email for a few years after that last visit - not often, but at marker events. She and her husband, not without major reproductive challenges, became parents of two children. I marveled at the family pictures she sent me, not just of her beautiful babies, but of her, so happy, present, vibrant, beaming with purpose. She also sent photos of her husband and of Belle, enjoying herself in the snow. Her practice was thriving, and life was sweet. Until I reached out to her in December 2019 to seek her permission to write about her in this book, we had not corresponded since the spring of 2012. Her sentences below, taken from that last email, are a fitting testimonial to healing and recovery.

"It blows my mind a little to think of how long I was under your care. It was such a huge significant chapter in my life and it now seems so far away, and when I think of that period of time, it's almost like it was about a different person. You know, I can't for the life of me remember when I last saw you. I mean, I remember the visit itself, down at Mercy Hospital, but I can't remember even what year that was. It just seems like so much time has passed. For so long, I think I was waiting to have an epiphany about my purpose in life and gain some great understanding about my failed relationship. For whatever reason, I was able to give 'life' another try. And with all its ups and downs, maybe it's just all part of 'life's rich pageant.' Anyway, I just needed you to know that I am okay, and that I will continue to be okay. And thank you again for your time, patience and caring over those many years.

Take good care, Jane."

Teaching

As I mentioned earlier, my career, until 2008, was always divided into half-time private practice and half-time academic work (teaching, administration and leadership, clinical research, and writing). I've always felt that both dimensions have been essential to me. Not only do they inform each other but my professional growth is a result of what I've learned from my patients in my private practice and from my students and colleagues in the academy. During my mid-career years, my teaching took off – exponentially! In addition to my didactic teaching at the medical school and clinical teaching at the hospital, I was now on the road quite frequently, giving lectures nationally and internationally. As a sample, my diary for 1998 lists forty-seven out-of-town presentations, for 1999 forty-six, for 2000 thirty-nine, and for 2001 thirty-nine again. Fortunately, I was often able to piggyback these invited talks onto annual medical meetings of associations I belonged to and was attending for other reasons — such as continuing medical education, committee assignments, or various administrative duties. And most of these meetings were over weekends, which also helped me maintain weekday commitments to my patients and trainees.

But it wouldn't be entirely forthcoming for me to say that it was seamless. As I alluded to above in my treatment of Jane, being a doctors' doctor conveys a serious and moral responsibility. You can't be out of town all the time and practice safe and competent psychiatry. I didn't have the benefits of telemedicine/telepsychiatry over those years, but cell phone therapy was essential at times. And my day timer. Being organized was essential. Ditto for the support of key people in my life. My colleagues at the hospital and the partners in my private practice were generous and steadfast. My wife and kids were amazing. I was so thankful that their lives were busy, too; this assuaged my guilt. And, we were careful to intersperse long weekends and relaxing vacations into the mix.

A lovely anecdote about one of my patients. The first time I ran for president of the Canadian Psychiatric Association, I learned early one morning that I had lost the election. A few minutes later, I was walking with my first patient of the day from the waiting room to my office. She was a psychiatrist, and this was probably her third or fourth visit. Being a member of the CPA, she knew that I was running. She asked: "Have you heard the results of the election yet?" I said yes, and told her that I'd lost. "Thank god!" she blurted out. I started to laugh, and so did she. By this time, the office door was closed. She continued: "Well, that certainly wasn't very sympathetic of me, was it? But let's be honest, I mean it. I need you. You know what a mess my life is in at the moment. You're my doctor. I want your help. These weekly visits are my lifeline." And with that, our session began. Fifty minutes later, after engaging with her and finishing up, I felt good, fulfilled, that I had been helpful. My disappointment in having lost the election was gone. I was struck by how my loss paled into insignificance when compared to what my patient was dealing with, a not uncommon sentiment in all of us who work in the mental health field.

Traveling

In addition to traveling to give lectures or other forms of teaching, I was also occupied with leadership responsibilities during this time. In the late 1990s and early 2000s, I was active in the American Psychiatric Association. I represented western Canada in the APA's assembly for a number of years and attended national meetings every fall and spring. The agenda was always filled with issues that impact our patients, their families, our students and our members. I gained experience and confidence as well in governance and policy, which culminated in my being elected to the Board of Trustees of the APA in 1997, a position I held for three years. This was an exciting time. It is an honor to have a voice in representing your constituents, to be their mouthpiece at a national level, and to bring back the results of our deliberations to the benefit of patients and colleagues alike.

Through it all, I never lost sight of my other identity, that of being a doctors' doctor. Sitting in the boardroom at APA headquarters in Washington, or at a town hall meeting, or in the hotel ballroom of a governance meeting far from home, physician health was always in the back of my mind. I asked myself in what ways this particular issue or position paper might affect the wellbeing of practicing physicians. Later, when I was appointed to the Board of Directors and the Editorial Board of American Psychiatric Association Publishing, my focus didn't waver. The mission was no longer governance but rather books and monographs. My editorial eye honed in on proposals and manuscripts that would not only convey new scientific information to psychiatrists but also appeal to their hearts and minds. And by extension, help their patients, including their doctor-patients for those who treat physicians.

In the fall of 2000, I became president of the Canadian Psychiatric Association, and my theme was "New Century: Overcoming Stigma/Respecting Differences." This was the busiest year of my life. Being on an airplane almost every other week was only a part of that. I took advantage of the enormous privilege of leading my national organization, and I was quite deliberate in outlining what I might realistically accomplish in those twelve short months. But, three months before I began my term, a tragedy occurred that deeply affected me and shaped my presidential year. I wrote about it in my first post to the membership, in October of 2000:

"'It's so sad. It's so sad' screamed the headline of The Globe and Mail, *Saturday August 12, 2000. And, thus began the account of the final hours of Dr. Suzanne Killinger-Johnson and her six-month-old son Cuyler which culminated in her leaping in front of a subway train in Toronto. Her son died immediately, Dr. Killinger-Johnson several days later. This horrific event has not only shocked and saddened the Canadian public but has also wounded the Canadian physician workforce.*

"As your new president, I begin with this story of loss and sorrow to reach out to all of you who belong to the Canadian Psychiatric Association. We are a diverse group of men and women who have come together with a common purpose: to provide a strong, collective voice for psychiatrists across the country and to foster a community dedicated to ensuring the highest possible standard of professional practice in providing psychiatric services to Canadians. Will we do anything differently after this? I believe so. Suicide isn't done in a vacuum – it affects a lot of people."[1]

I did not know Dr. Killinger-Johnson, but she was believed to be suffering from a postpartum illness, the magnitude of which had eluded her family and the Toronto police. I was interviewed by the national press and said the following: "This type of tragedy could happen to any human being… but when a physician is depressed, he or she suffers an even greater degree of guilt, shame, failure and the isolation that goes with that."[2] I added that it was also possible that the fact she was a physician aggravated her depression. And in my column to the membership, I called upon my colleagues in diverse fields – brain researchers, reproductive psychiatrists, mood disorder specialists, suicide researchers, psychotherapy experts – to continue their cutting-edge work and also lobby for funding to expand their output. I reminded those working in physician health to redouble their efforts at fighting the damaging effects of stigma when doctors become mentally ill, and to make themselves immediately available when a medical colleague knocks on their door.

One of the accomplishments during my presidential year was creating the Section on Physician Health of the CPA. Its intention was to complement the pioneering work of the Center for Physician Health of the Canadian Medical Association, but with a particular emphasis on the mental health vulnerabilities of physicians. I felt great pride in this initiative, and a measure of gratitude to the Board of Directors of CPA that they supported its formation. Four years earlier, when I wrote the CPA position paper "Treatment of the Mentally Ill Physician,"[3] I had inwardly hoped for this but put it aside. Hence, I could hardly contain my excitement when the new Section on Physician Health launched its first workshop "Melancholia in physicians: how can philosophy help?" at the annual meeting on November 17, 2001 in Montreal. The workshop was first thing in the morning, well attended, and just before my presidential address. A big day, and one I'll never forget.

I began my address with an expression of thanks to all the people who had supported me – my family, my work colleagues, the staff of CPA, and one other group. Here is what I said:

"One final thank-you: I must thank my patients. And, I want to do this publicly. Thank you for your generosity when I have had to cancel appointments at short notice, when because of a conference call or a quick trip to Ottawa, I have had to shift your appointments to early in the day, late in the day, or a Saturday. Thanks for your gracious understanding of my quest to extend my reach beyond the fifty-minute hour."

It was more than a heartfelt thank-you to each of my doctor-patients in Vancouver for being flexible and accommodating - I needed them to know that I couldn't have accomplished so much in that year without them. That their personal narratives, their suffering and struggle, their fortitude and forbearance had become part of me and pushed me to lengths that I didn't realize were within. I was fiercely clear that Dr. Suzanne Killinger-Johnson and her son Cuyler would not die in vain. That out of the ashes of tragedy would come change and discovery. And I felt a similar kind of passion for all my patients, that I was in a privileged position for one year, and I could fight for them and do my part to ease their burden. And this is why I chose to end my talk with a disguised story from my practice:[4]

"I want to conclude with a story. A simple story, but so complex and textured. A story that speaks to my presidential theme. A story about stigma and about difference. A story of love. A story about loss and confusion. A story about humility and unworthiness. A story of sadness and hope. A story of connection and healing, countertransference, and the often-sacred nature of our work:

"It was a Monday morning and I was at the hospital. The telephone rang and the caller was a specialist on staff. He is an International

Medical Graduate and both an ethnic and religious minority physician. His words were: 'Dr. Myers, I'm sorry to bother you, but I would like your advice. My son... my son... my son died two weeks ago, he committed suicide. I'm not feeling well... I don't know if that's normal or not... I'm just wondering if I should talk to someone... this is new for me, I haven't had to face this before... I'm sorry to bother you... I know how busy you are.' I can't remember my exact words of response, but his words are etched in my memory. I said: 'What are you doing right now?' He replied: 'Talking to you.' I said: 'Come down to my office in fifteen minutes.' I asked my resident to supervise my medical student with her patient so that I could meet with this man, and we began our therapeutic work together.

"As you will all understand, Dr. H's grief was profound and ever present. He was open and expressive - he filled each visit with happy memories and sad memories, regrets and 'if-onlys,' lost opportunities, his search for answers, his sense of failure as a dad, and his unrelenting guilt and self-blame. Lots of tears and lots of angry outbursts. On the third visit with me, he brought in a picture of his son Kam. I gazed at this fine-looking young man, eyes bright, his smile big and full of promise. Later in the visit, Dr. H began describing a painful intrusive flashback he had been having. It was the horrific image of Kam hanging from a crossbeam on the deck of his apartment, where Dr. H found him. He went on to describe cutting Kam down, performing CPR - to no avail - and then holding his six-foot-four-inch son in his arms and gently rocking him and singing a lullaby in his native tongue, a soothing song from his infancy. My eyes filled with tears as I watched him. I listened and sat quietly.

Thank you. Merci beaucoup."

As I looked out at the audience, and as my colleagues began to stand and applaud, I basked in the warmth of the moment. I was aware that I had just done what most psychiatrists in leadership do not do - share a story from their practice. By speaking about Dr. H so publicly, I wanted to highlight, and give an example of, what goes on behind closed doors in all therapists' offices. And how privileged we are as psychiatrists to do the kind of work we do. I had Dr. H's permission to do this. When I next met with him back in Vancouver, I thanked him again. His modest and humble reply was: "Kam and I both hope that our story helps others."

Another Dimension of the Middle Years

In 2001, I was approached by one of the editors of the publication *Physician's Money Digest*, to write a column on the marriages of physicians. I leapt at the opportunity, and for the next six years, until 2007, penned a piece each month. I called it "How's Your Marriage, Doctor?"

I will explain more about this in the following chapter.

References

1. Michael F. Myers, "Suicide: From Despair to Hope," President's Pen, *The Bulletin of the Canadian Psychiatric Association*. (October 2000): 133-34.

2. Cheryl Hawkes, "So much to live for: Doctors confront the myth of their invulnerability," *Maclean's* (August 28, 2000): 39.

3. Michael F. Myers, "Treatment of the mentally ill physician," Canadian Psychiatric Association Position Paper, *The Canadian Journal of Psychiatry* 42(6) (1997): 1-6.

4. Michael F. Myers, Presidential Address. "New Century: Overcoming Stigma, Respecting Differences," Presidential Address, *The Canadian Journal of Psychiatry* 46(12) (2001): 907-14.

Chapter Six

Treating Physicians and Their Marriages

"Love cures people - both the ones who give it and the ones who receive it."

Dr. Karl A. Menninger, American psychiatrist, and founder of the Menninger Foundation and the Menninger Clinic, Topeka, Kansas.

I began to see couples, including doctors and their spouses or partners, early in my career. This also involved teaching couples' therapy to students and residents, and publishing papers and books on the subject. What I would like to convey in this chapter is how much I learned about physicians by examining their intimate relationships - the strengths and the struggles, the ease and the dis-ease, the agony and the ecstasy. I believe that my becoming a doctors' doctor was both informed and conditioned by having a window into these most private dimensions of their being. A psychiatrist who offers couples' therapy was unusual then – and still is. Most marital therapists are non-medical practitioners, such as psychologists and clinical social workers. Parallels to this I've seen in other branches of medicine are general surgeons who do colonoscopies, primary care physicians who assist surgeons in the operating room, and gynecologists and urologists who provide sex therapy.

Couples' Therapy as the Route to Care

It is never easy for physicians to pick up the phone and call for help, but the vast majority eventually do, especially when their symptoms become unbearable or frightening. But even in this group, there are doctors who dig in their heels, ferociously. Sooner or later, their marriage is impacted because their spouse cannot cope with the withdrawal or irritability that accompanies professional burnout or untreated depression. Or the absence and/or egocentricity that accompanies unchecked alcohol abuse. Or the social restriction and dependency that accompanies untreated anxiety and phobias. It's at this point that couples therapy is suggested by the spouse; if the response is repeatedly negative, the message becomes a threat: "Either you go with me to see someone or I'm outa here." Here's an example:[1]

"'Dr. Myers, this is Mrs. Jones calling. Will you see my husband and me? I've given him an ultimatum – marital therapy or else I'm leaving. I'll explain when we see you in person.' I arranged a visit for Mrs. and Dr. Jones the following week. Here are a few opening remarks:

"Mrs. Jones: 'I'm dying inside. It's loneliness. I thought I was lonely before I got married. This is ten times as bad. My husband doesn't talk.

I'm living with a stranger. Some days I think my head is going to burst — with rage. Other days I can't stop crying.'

"Dr. Jones: 'Irma is right. I'm not a talker. I've always been quiet and inward. I feel badly that she's so unhappy. Maybe we made a mistake getting married. I didn't know the ground rules.'*

"I asked a few questions and learned a lot. Mrs. Jones was a landscape architect and Dr. Jones a pathologist. They were the same age, 36, and they had been married for three years. This was a first marriage for each. They met online and were married nine months later. Communication was not a problem at the beginning. Talking had slowly diminished over the last eighteen months or so. There did not seem to be a particular stressor or recent event in either of their personal or professional lives that might have triggered this.

"'And I don't think I'm depressed either' said Dr. Jones. 'Irma has asked me about that — and whether I'm having an affair — which I'm not.'*

"I scheduled individual visits with each of them. It's my visit with Dr. Jones that I want to highlight. He was correct that he wasn't depressed, in a clinical sense, but was he sad, preoccupied and broken? Yes — and for good reasons. Dr. Jones' background was punctuated with loss. When he was 11 years old, his only sibling, an older sister died of Reye's syndrome. This was devastating for his parents, especially his mother who had administered aspirin to his sister during a bout of chicken pox.

"'My mom never recovered after Tanya's death. The light went out of her eyes. I never heard her laugh again. She never forgave herself. Psychiatrists tried hard to help her with antidepressants and therapy but nothing seemed to work. What happened next is so very hard to talk about. I lost both my mom and dad together. My mother hanged herself seventeen years ago. Five days later, just after her funeral and as I got off the plane returning to college, the police greeted me with the news that my father was dead. He shot himself in the heart on top of my mother's grave. I don't know how I survived this. I still don't.'

"Dr. Jones was willing to begin individual therapy with me and this was very helpful. He had never truly examined the impact of losing his entire family — and so violently. After only a few sessions, Mrs. Jones began to see changes in him. He became more animated and open with her. They slowly regained intimacy. I met with him weekly for about one year. Marital therapy was not necessary."

Dr. Jones was pleased that he sought help. He told me that he never considered seeing a mental health professional because he basically coped well as a doctor and enjoyed a quiet personal life, but that he knew his losses were "more than the average person." What he didn't realize, however, was how much he had been oppressed by the weight of his aggregate loss. His therapy was essentially grief work. He needed to recognize and release a panoply of emotion that was deeply buried. He mentioned, and both his wife and I noticed, a change in his gait and his facial animation. Dr. Jones told me that he found himself whistling again. He had not whistled since he was 11 years old, just before Tanya's death.

How Individual Treatment Improves the Medical Marriage

What follows is an example of a couple where getting the physician into care was both convoluted and challenging. Though unfortunately this case is not rare, it illustrates how many doctors determinedly fight against becoming patients.

Mrs. Anto, the wife of an internist, was referred to me several years ago by her family physician who was concerned about her drinking. I diagnosed her with alcohol dependence, moderately severe major depressive disorder and a significant marital problem. Her alcoholism was quite entrenched. Despite assessment and follow up by an addiction medicine physician, trials of disulfiram, regular attendance at Alcoholics Anonymous, a step group for women, a sponsor and four weeks of residential care, Mrs. Anto found it hard to maintain sobriety. She did get her one-year cake at AA, but when her husband didn't show up, she relapsed. To her credit, she regained her sobriety quickly, but it always seemed tenuous. Antidepressant medication kept her mood disorder largely at bay but she was not a happy woman.

Dr. Anto was a high-profile physician with a national and international reputation in his specialty. He adamantly refused to participate in his wife's treatment. When he was a "no show" at an early session with his wife, I called him at work and invited him to come in to meet with me alone. He demurred, thanked me for calling and effusively expressed his gratitude for my helping his wife. I felt that I had no recourse but to be cordial and leave the door open for him. Meanwhile, Mrs. Anto's complaints continued – that he was obsessed with his work and his hobbies of golf and coin collecting – and that she was desperately unhappy. Her loneliness was palpable. She told me that her husband was critical of my care (that she wasn't depressed and didn't need antidepressants) and the work of her addictions' specialist ("what does Dr. Jay know – he's in recovery himself?"). According to Mrs. Anto, her husband was against AA ("they just convert alcohol addiction to meeting addiction") and any therapy. He admits to being the son of an alcoholic himself and told her that all of that "adult children of alcoholics stuff, codependency, and enabling is BS." His prescription for her was to simply stop drinking. She expressed a fair amount of anger about him in her visits with me.

From a distance, I happened to see Dr. Anto at a large general medical conference, where we were both lecturing. He approached me when I was alone: "I can't thank you enough, Dr. Myers – Stella is doing so well." I said "Thanks... but I'm still worried about her – and the marriage – if you're uncomfortable meeting with me about that I understand – may I suggest a few good marital therapists in town?" Dr. Anto said: "That won't be necessary. I think Stella will be a much happier person once she's not drinking for a longer period. I find that to be true in my women patients who drink too much. Thanks again, Dr. Myers, enjoy the meeting!" And off he went.

One week later, Mrs. Anto overdosed after a fight with her husband. He called 911 and she was taken to Emergency. I assessed her, and after medical clearance, she was able to go home. But I got a chance to have a few minutes with the two of them before they left. Dr. Anto seemed embarrassed, but sincerely concerned. He agreed to come and see me with his wife, and this time he showed up. That visit proved pivotal. With my guidance, they were each able to get a lot off their chests, much of which they had never shared before in such a clear and heartfelt way. After I had an individual visit with Dr. Anto, the two of them and I embarked on a series of weekly visits and things improved markedly at home.

Dr. Anto harbored a secret that he told me about when I met with him alone. He had put himself on an antidepressant about three years earlier (he felt down about the state of his marriage and couldn't shake it off, he wasn't sleeping, and he was having trouble concentrating) and he had never told his wife about this. He felt flawed, ashamed and embarrassed that he "needed a crutch." This was why he was so negative about his wife taking medication, his criticism of her was simply a manifestation of his inner self-loathing. With my encouragement, he disclosed this in a session with the two of them together. This was a watershed moment in their therapy. He was upset, inarticulate and vulnerable as he described this to her. He looked frightened, diminished and lost. Mrs. Anto held him in her arms, soothing and comforting him as he wept. I sat quietly, witnessing their intimacy, recaptured after a long hiatus. After this session, Dr. Anto asked me if I'd be willing to see him for "a little personal help," which we agreed to do. This was a great help to him in dealing with his rage about his childhood and absent alcoholic father.

Speaking generally, there are many messages about physicians in Dr. Anto's story. One is that they set the bar high for themselves and cannot fathom any perceived blemish or flaw. Dr. Anto was upset with himself for getting depressed and "needing an antidepressant," so upset that he self-medicated surreptitiously rather than go to a doctor, get a proper diagnosis, and let that doctor treat him. Second, his wife's drinking embarrassed him, almost as if this were a slight on his self-image. But this came out both in his judgment and avoidance of her. Only her worsening and attempting to kill herself forced him to face how desperately unhappy and isolated Mrs. Anto felt. Third, it was only through the lens of his marriage that he could look inwardly and accept his personal woundedness. At first, he thought he was only in my office because of her drinking problem, that he was there to provide observations and give support. He soon came to realize that he was a participant too, and that it was safe to yield his defenses and come in touch with his humanness. Fourth, individual therapy enabled him to be more authentic, to know himself better, to have greater personal insight beyond his identity as "just a doctor." This process made him into a husband, someone whom his wife fell in love with, in ways she never imagined possible.

When Infidelity Is Rooted in Individual Illness

There are diverse reasons why one's spouse gets involved with someone else, and most marital therapists see a number of couples each year with this as the main reason they've sought professional help. Here's an example of a couple, both doctors, married for many years, who were in crisis mode when they called for help.[2]

"Dr. Bernice English and Dr. Hamilton Walsh came to see me a number of years ago. Dr. English was a rheumatologist and Dr. Walsh a cardiologist. They were both 60 years old and had been married for thirty-one years, having met during their residencies. They had three adult children, all doing well.

"Our saga is called 'Mopping up after the affair' began Dr. English. She started to cry. Dr. Walsh sat stone-faced at a distance from her on my couch. I passed her the box of Kleenex. Silence from both. I looked at them and said 'Do you want to talk about it?' More silence. Finally, Dr. Walsh spoke, but not before receiving non-verbal permission from his

wife. 'Bernice had a brief fling with her golf instructor recently — it's over now — but I'm worried about her, Dr. Myers — I'm afraid she might harm herself.' I looked at Dr. English — she averted her gaze. 'I don't deserve to live — this is so painful — I've brought shame on my family, my reputation, my profession — I hate myself, I want Hamilton to divorce me.'

"As the interview continued, I learned some key information. Dr. English's relationship with the other man seemed in part due to a lapse of judgment. This behavior was certainly out of character for her. She had a history of mental illness, having suffered untreated postpartum depression after her second and third children. 'What did we know in those days? I just thought that I was inadequate and weak — my mother told me that I was too much a career woman and not enough of a nurturer. My guilt was off the wall. Hamilton was wonderful — so was our nanny — I couldn't have survived without them. It was only later when I was feeling normal again that I told Hamilton how suicidal I had been — it went on for weeks.' She denied any recurrence of depression since — until now, which she attributed to the affair.

"But something else came out in that first visit. Dr. English's father had suffered from bipolar illness as did his brother and a cousin. 'And I think you've got a touch of it yourself, dear' said Dr. Walsh. He continued: 'Ever since your menopause, you go up and down in your spirits, not wildly but subtly for weeks at a time. You've been on a high since about March (it was now July) — you're up earlier than usual, playing your music loudly, wearing more makeup, taking on more responsibilities at the hospital. Although our garden is stunning this year, your planting has been a bit excessive. And you're obsessed with golf — even before you got involved with Derek I was worried about you — I've never seen you flirt so much in all the years we've been married.'

"I met with Dr. English individually for the remainder of the visit and again the next day. My diagnosis was bipolar illness, type II. She was very depressed but not actively suicidal. I put her on medical leave – I felt that she was not well enough to be working. She responded nicely to both a mood stabilizer and an antidepressant medication and returned to her regular and habitual state of mind and functioning. After about six weeks, she was well enough to return to work. She remained stable for the rest of the time that I was her psychiatrist.

"My visits with the two of them were largely supportive and educational. They had a strong marital infrastructure and loved each other deeply. I also met with their children – they were worried about their mother's up-and-down moods, and were relieved to see her so well. They had no knowledge of their mother's indiscretion – I agreed with both Dr. English and Dr. Walsh that disclosing this was not necessary. Their intergenerational boundaries with their kids were healthy and needed to be kept that way."

These two doctors came for marital therapy, but they didn't have a marital problem in the conventional sense, where the marriage is the "patient" in need of professional help. Although Dr. English called it "mopping up after the affair," and yes, that was a part of it, what seemed most important was uncovering the dynamic that drove the extramarital dalliance. Having Dr. Walsh in the room was invaluable, and my job was made easier not only by how articulate and insightful each was but how loving and mature they were. Dr. Walsh was able to use his training and knowledge of basic psychiatry in a healthy and constructive way, putting forward his hunch that his wife had an illness that lowered her inhibitions and caused her to stray. This protected him from the intense emotions of betrayal, anger, mistrust and humiliation so common when one's spouse violates the marital bond. These feelings were present but tempered by his worry about her mental health. Dr. English's guilt, self-loathing and despair were largely helped with medication and psychotherapy, but her husband's love and commitment to the marriage cannot be underestimated in her journey of recovery. Now that she had a diagnosis, Dr. English also benefited from the affectionate behavior of her adult children, who were relieved that their longstanding concerns about their mother were now allayed. All three of them were open to learning as much as they could about bipolar illness and welcomed my suggestions.

What's Love Got to Do with It?

I am borrowing the title of Tina Turner's iconic 1984 song to introduce this section. The words of Dr. Menninger, quoted earlier in this chapter, speak to physicians in general and to physicians as spouses. It is my premise that physicians who seem the happiest in love have been able to most successfully integrate the responsibilities of their work and their intimate relationships at home. No easy task.

Many doctors are wounded healers. Because of early trauma and loss, like family breakup, death or sickness of a parent, physical, sexual or emotional abuse, forced migration, childhood illness while growing up, these same women and men may have difficulty finding – but more often sustaining – mature love in their intimate relationships. Medical school gives ascendancy to science, intellectualization and rationalism – it devalues emotion and the importance of love in the hearts of its students. The culture of medicine demands "objectivity" and "clinical neutrality" in its practitioners. In many physicians this character armor sticks like glue, and it is carried from the workplace into the home. Giving and receiving love in the medical marriage becomes a challenge. Here's an example:

"Dr. Glen, a 44-year-old thoracic surgeon, consulted me about four weeks after his wife left him. He did not see it coming. She, on the other hand, argued that she had been trying to tell him for years that she was unhappy, lonely and bored in the marriage - he worked long hours and maintained a range of medically-related interests outside of his clinical work. She said that he never listened to her unhappy pleas for change or her wish to go with him for marital therapy. A few months before she left she met another man at work and started a relationship with him.

"Dr. Glen was intensely mourning the loss of his wife. He told me about an incident that occurred in the operating room the previous week. Suddenly, he experienced a wave of sorrow come over him, and his eyes filled with tears - a classical feature of grief when someone loses a person dear to them. When one of the nurses asked if he was okay, he replied: 'Yes, I think I've developed an allergy to this new disinfectant they're using here in the OR.' It passed. When he was recounting this story in my office, he said to me that he wished he could blurt out to the whole surgical team: 'My eyes are like this because I can't stop crying - my wife is gone - my heart is broken!' Reflecting, Dr. Glen then said to me: 'But how acceptable is that in the middle of a lung resection?'" [3]

This is an example of lost love in the medical marriage. How the demands of sick patients and one doctor's love of his work blinded him to another kind of love – that of a spouse. This story also illustrates how tough it is to have a normal grief reaction and still do your job – especially if you are a male surgeon.

Dr. Glen was my patient a long time ago. My hope is that male surgeons today, faced with the abrupt loss of a beloved wife, would not have to lie about their tears in the operating room. Their grief would be just as raw but at least they could give vent to their sorrow without deception or embarrassment.

A Gay Male Couple

Working with same-sex couples is very gratifying and even more so when one or both are physicians. The contemporary acceptance of gayness, including gay marriage, is still relatively new, and this includes the house of medicine. Most medical students today are open, but some of their professors and clinical supervisors are, at best, only selectively out to immediate colleagues and friends. Creating a safe atmosphere for gay doctors with marital problems to come for therapy is essential. This lessens the oppression of "otherness" that so many live with. [4]

"Whether we split up or stay together, we need help' said Dr. Tang over the phone. I made an appointment for him and his partner. In my first visit, I learned that he was 42, divorced, father of a nine-year-old son, and an associate professor of surgery. His partner, Dr. Hay, stated: 'And I'm 30, a chief resident in nephrology, and tired of being bossed around – both at work and at home.' And that set the tone of the session. Dr. Tang did most of the talking. Dr. Hay sat largely silently but spoke volumes with his body language and expressive facial gestures.

"This was the first same-sex relationship for each of them. They had been coupled for four years, having met at a medical conference. Dr. Tang had been out of his marriage for about two years at that time – he and his wife divorced as a result of his coming out as gay. Dr. Hay was newly out and this was a significant dynamic in their troubled relationship. He liked to party 'occasionally,' to hang out with single gay men his age 'occasionally,' and to take E (ecstasy) 'occasionally.' Dr. Tang reacted to all of this in a highly controlled manner with pedantic lectures and diatribes on fidelity, ascetic self-denial, and Internet literature searches on the medical dangers of MDMA.

"But their relationship had additional challenges. In an individual visit with Dr. Hay, I learned that he had a significant history of untreated and recurrent depression – including a suicide gesture in college. He was actually quite worried about his potential for self-harm. I diagnosed him with a persistent depressive disorder and he improved significantly with an antidepressant. Specifically, he slept better, was less irritable, felt more self-worth, and became a little more assertive. Unfortunately, he developed sexual side-effects with the medication and this posed more anxiety for Dr. Tang. Viagra helped.

"Another complication was the interracial and interfaith issue. No problem for the two of them but it was for their families. I found it interesting – and refreshing – that both Dr. Tang's and Dr. Hay's families were accepting of their gayness. But it seems that each family had hoped that their son would commit to a man of his own race and religion. I was able to make suggestions of how to talk to their families in a calmer and less defensive way. It was heartwarming to learn how well Dr. Hay got along with Dr. Tang's son and vice-versa – and what a significant presence the boy was in their family.

"The two of them made great strides with therapy. There was a thorny 'father-son' element that needed to end. I spent time helping Dr. Tang recognize his feelings – insecurity about their age difference, fears of being abandoned, anger, and loneliness – and to speak about these emotions directly with Dr. Hay. His manner become less intellectual and softer – and more genuine. Dr. Hay gained insight into his passive-aggressive ways, and he too began to speak more openly and clearly to Dr. Tang when he was upset and felt like 'rebelling.' As things improved at home, Dr. Hay tired of the club scene and the two of them found many ways of having fun together as a couple - and with their friends."

Not captured here is how much each of them benefited from individual therapy. I ended up seeing each of them weekly for a while, interspersing a conjoint visit every six weeks or so. This worked nicely and after about nine or ten months we were done. Their way of communicating with each other worked effectively, enabling each of them to feel heard and respected. Any power difference, originally felt to be rooted in their age gap, dissipated. Interestingly, as they felt tighter and stronger as a couple and blended family, each of their families seemed to relax and accept their diversity.

A Lesbian Couple

"Drs. Emily Stone and Sue Garcia called asking for 'urgent help.' They were a married lesbian couple with twin sons, age nine months. Here is what I learned in their first visit. Dr. Stone was an endocrinologist and Dr. Garcia a primary care physician in a women's health clinic. Dr. Garcia was impregnated by donor insemination and learned early on by ultrasound that she was carrying twins. Both Dr. Garcia and Dr. Stone

were happy about that and their boys were delivered by caesarian section at 36 weeks. Dr. Garcia took an extended maternity leave so that she could be home full-time. Dr. Stone took a month off and then returned to her busy academic and clinical practice. This is when trouble began.

"'It's like I've been abandoned' complained Dr. Garcia. 'I am so angry. I get no support at all. I'm exhausted all the time. Whenever Emily is home, I do one of two things – dump the boys on her and collapse in bed or start bitching at her. I've turned into one of those miserable, depressed housewives like I used to see in my practice. Their husbands leave each day for work and then come home complaining how tired they are. Give me a break.' Dr. Stone then spoke: 'I agree with part one but not part two. You have turned into a bitter woman and it's hard living with you. I'm afraid to call you during the day because I can't seem to say anything that makes you feel better. I dread coming home. But I resent your saying that I complain I'm tired. When have I said that? You know I think that looking after Jake and Brad is much harder work than mine. And I try to pitch in as much as I can.'

"A quick synopsis of the help that I offered. More history and time spent with each of them confirmed my hunch that Dr. Garcia was clinically depressed. She agreed to antidepressant medication but only once she completed weaning the boys. I met with her alone for a few visits – she needed simple support and validation that she was a good mother and partner and that she would feel happy again. Dr. Stone had a sabbatical coming up in two months, which freed her up to both assist and bond with Jake and Brad. Dr. Garcia decided to return to work starting at two days per week. Her mother agreed to help out. I suggested a part-time nanny as well, which they both resisted, arguing: 'That's so heterosexist – surely two mothers and a grandmother can cope with twins?' I replied *with a little laughter: 'Call it heterosexist if you like, but twins are work. And what about all the other things like laundry, food shopping, cooking and more? And what about your relationship? You two need more time together, time to relax and to get out as a couple and have fun.'"* [5]

The key lesson of this story, and its successful outcome, is that I got this couple talking again, which renewed their faith in each other and their beautiful family.

When It's Too Late for Marital Therapy

Although this chapter is about treating physicians and their marriages, I've added a story about a young doctor here who I saw only on his own. His ticket to care, like the surgeon above, was precipitated by the demise of his marriage. And this point of entry - where a patient has their first exposure to psychotherapy - is common in newly-separated people. What this example also speaks to is that it often takes a big loss or stressful matter in a doctor's life for them to devote and protect the time for working on themselves and not overworking at medicine. [6]

"'Greetings Dr. Myers, this is Dr. Beck calling. I'd like to come to see you. I came home from work the other night to a Dear John letter. I'm pretty upset.' I responded with one of my unconscious, gut reactions: 'Ouch... I'm sorry to hear that... sure, let me get my appointment book... how about tomorrow at 6 p.m.?'

"Dr. Beck was a young nephrologist in town. I remembered him from his medical student days when he spent his psychiatry clerkship with me at the teaching hospital where I worked. I also remembered his wife,

Dr. Ames — she did her clerkship there, too. She had gone on to become a family physician. My memory of them was that they were a striking couple — both good-looking, smart, well-liked and talented musically. And they did marathons together. I wondered what happened? Why did Dr. Ames move out like that — gone — with just a note of goodbye? Were they still running marathons? And if so, did she literally 'run' away from her marriage?

"Dr. Beck was more than upset. He was a wreck - absolutely devastated that his wife was gone. He told me that they'd had one visit with a marital therapist about two weeks previously. Dr. Ames did not see any merit in returning to the psychologist because they were too busy. Dr. Beck told her that was 'a crock.' And he told me that therapy is frightening to his wife. He thought that it was rooted in her growing-up years. 'She was forced to see a psychiatrist when she was a kid - she had a long bout of anorexia and bulimia' he said. Her parents were unhappily married, her mother attempted suicide a number of times, and was eventually diagnosed with bipolar illness. They went on to divorce when Dr. Ames was away at college. During her first year of medical school, Dr. Ames' mother killed herself. It was shortly after this painful loss that she met Dr. Beck.

"'My background is no bed of roses either, Dr. Myers,' said Dr. Beck. 'I'm an adult child of two alcoholics — both my mother and father were big drinkers. Both doctors. My mother got help though and has been dry and with AA for five years. My dad still drinks — but less. He loves his denial. He's very self-righteous. My brother has had problems with cocaine — he's been twice to residential care — dad never visited him. My folks have a lousy marriage. See why, with my wife's background and mine, it's so important to me to make my marriage work?'

"Dr. Beck told me more about his relationship. They both worked hard and played hard. They had lots of friends, kept active and enjoyed sharing many community events. But they didn't talk easily together, except for everyday matters. They had decided not to have children – this seemed mutual and was related to their upbringing. It was only in the past year that Dr. Beck sensed that his wife was pulling away. She had made a number of independent friends – all single or divorced – whom she preferred to see on her own. She was less communicative at home, '...more private and kind of touchy when I probed.' Their sexual relationship had fallen off to zero the past few months. 'Of course, I suspected an affair' said Dr. Beck. However, Dr. Ames denied it and he let it drop.

"What helped this young doctor? I met individually with him for over a year. He needed to talk about being abandoned, the frustration of not being given a chance to fight for his marriage, and, failing that, the opportunity to unravel their marriage together. His self-esteem was poor. He gained important insights into his loneliness and other wounds from childhood, and how he became a caretaker – not just professionally but initially of his wife, too. Our work together ended when he began group therapy with other physicians seeking to understand themselves better."

I never saw Dr. Beck again as a patient, but he did send me a note about six or seven years later. He wanted me to know that he attended the group for about two years and had benefited considerably from it. He talked about becoming a more spiritual person, taking up yoga, and attending meditation retreats. He was dating off and on, but was "not rushing into anything." He was happy with his life.

Summing Up

These disguised examples from my practice illustrate many things. One, the diversity of women and men who are physicians. Two, the ways in which marital strain has a direct interplay with one's ability to practice medicine and vice-versa. Three, that physicians are much more complex than their professional role and image. And four, physicians are no different than other people. They too are subject to life's challenges and curveballs. And shining a light on, and exploring, their intimate relationships can be both illuminating and healing.

References

1. Michael F. Myers, "How's Your Marriage, Doctor?" Physician's Money Digest, (June 2006): md-mag.com. https://www.mdmag.com/journals/pmd/2006/109/4715

2. Ibid. February 15, 2005 https://www.mdmag.com/journals/pmd/2005/83/3733

3. Ibid. July 31, 2003. https://www.mdmag.com/journals/pmd/2003/56

4. Ibid. March 15, 2003. https://www.mdmag.com/journals/pmd/2003/49/3536

5. Ibid. https://www.mdmag.com/journals/pmd/

6. Ibid. February 15, 2004 https://www.mdmag.com/journals/pmd/2004/28/1908

Chapter Seven

Losing a Doctor to Suicide

The time of day is about eight o'clock in the morning as I'm in my car driving to the hospital where I work. Lots of traffic, as usual. Light turns amber. Rather than speeding up and trying to cross the intersection, I actually slow down and come to a stop just as the light turns red. There's a Starbuck's at the corner to my right. I see Dr. Z, sitting outside, enjoying the morning sun with his coffee and a cigarette. He's alone. He can't see me, we're at right angles to each other. Dark glasses hide his eyes. He's not on his cellphone or reading the morning paper or a book. He's quite still, looking straight ahead. As I gaze at him, I wonder what's going through his mind. I draw a parallel with the way he sits and waits for me in my waiting room, minus the coffee and cigarette, plus or minus the dark glasses. My fixation on him is jarred by the car behind me, the driver honking his horn. The light has turned green. I continue on my journey, but Dr. Z remains in my mind's eye. Less than three weeks later, he will kill himself.

I have chosen to devote this entire chapter to my work with Dr. Z. My relationship with him goes to the heart of my becoming a doctors' doctor. Losing a patient to suicide is known to be one of the most stressful experiences in the professional lives of psychiatrists and other mental health professionals. Fearing this, certain psychiatrists try to avoid treating patients at risk of taking their own lives; others, so traumatized by the suicide of a patient, retire or leave clinical work altogether to focus instead on research and teaching. As I mentioned earlier in this memoir, it's suicide and its devastation that drew me to the field. And when I became aware that we physicians are at higher risk of suicide than the general population, that made me even more committed to helping my colleagues in need.

I attempted, successfully, to locate Dr. Z's sister who has graciously given me permission to tell his story. It is almost twenty-five years since he died. She is highly aware of the stigma in the medical world attached to suicide and is unequivocally supportive of the airing of her brother's struggle and sad outcome. And that attitudes need to change. What follows is a modestly disguised accounting of the truth. Although I've kept his complete file in my possession, I'm being vague on dates here. I've left out highly personal revelations that were for my eyes only and not necessary for the substance of this chapter, and I've changed genders and added deliberate distracting details at times. I'm hoping that no one will feel offended or harmed by this account - on the contrary, my wish is for Dr. Z's life to be honored and respected. As will become obvious, Dr. Z was open with his family and medical colleagues about his psychiatric illnesses and his treatment. And while being under my care in a teaching hospital, not once did he refuse to talk to or be interviewed by medical students or residents in training. He was kind-hearted, generous, and committed to medical education.

Background

Dr. Z was in his forties when he first came to see me in the 1990s. It was his family doctor who, privy to the issues that Dr. Z was sharing with him, convinced him that he might benefit from seeing a psychiatrist. "I don't like myself, one bit, and despite my accomplishments, I feel like a failure" was how he started his first visit with me. He was always a good student and functioned well in his first career as a teacher. He was an older, non-traditional applicant to medical school, and was a recent graduate and second-year resident in physical and rehabilitative medicine when I met him. He recalled thinking that he might be developing a depression even before starting medical school, but, like so many medical students and doctors, he pushed himself harder and harder and just carried on. Six weeks or so before I saw him, he felt much worse. His energy was zapped, he never slept more than three hours at a shot, he was losing weight, and for the first time in his life he found himself churning about ways that he might kill himself.

Dr. Z was straightforward with me about how much he was drinking to try to deal with his insomnia, but he was insightful enough to know that at the end of the day alcohol was making him feel worse. Being a physician with knowledge of what defines the illness of depression, he rattled off a list of the symptoms and signs, all of which clinched the diagnosis. He agreed to start an antidepressant and, at my suggestion and admonition, to scale back his daily drinking, ideally stop completely in the short term. So far so good. His sleep improved almost immediately and within two weeks his mood began to lift. After another six to eight weeks, he told me that he felt about 75 percent improved. He was pleased and so was I. He admitted to "an occasional" glass of wine, but no more than this, and no hard liquor, which had been what he was drinking earlier.

Dr. Z told me in the first visit that he was struggling with his sexual orientation, and had been for years. "I wonder if I'm gay… I'm attracted to other guys but I've never done anything about it." On the advice of his family doctor, he had just begun psychotherapy with a gay-affirming therapist. He was a bit wary and ambivalent: "What if I find out that I really am gay? That scares the shit out of me. But I guess I could get my head around that as long as I don't have to get intimate with anyone. I suppose I could lead a celibate life. That's okay, isn't it?" I didn't answer his question directly, but said: "Sounds like your question is about not having to rock the boat on how you've been leading your life, on your own, alone." He agreed, but responded with something both existential and familial: "There's so much pressure to be coupled in our society, and it seems to get worse as I get older." He had more to say and I just listened.

He continued to see his therapist on a regular basis and enrolled in a "coming out" group for gay men. He was no longer seeing me that often as he was stable on his medication. As the months wore on, he missed a visit, then returned several weeks later, in not good shape. He had gone off his medication and was drinking again. He didn't look well, he had a tremor, he cried repeatedly during the visit, and many of his depressive symptoms had returned. When I asked about suicidal thinking, he admitted that he had felt drawn to and tempted to steal potassium chloride (a commonly known means of suicide among doctors) from the hospital. I put him on medical leave. We repeated the drill - stop drinking, go back on the medication. I met with him briefly every few days, but this time he couldn't stop the alcohol. I got him assessed quickly by an addiction medicine specialist who recommended immediate admission to residential treatment. He reluctantly agreed.

But the night before he was to leave, he attempted suicide. And it was serious. While sitting in his car in a closed garage with the engine running, he downed two bottles of wine and swallowed his remaining antidepressant pills, though only a few because I was careful to prescribe him no more than two-week allotments. Fortunately, a passerby walking his dog, and feeling suspicious, investigated and called 911. He was taken to a local ER and after twenty-four hours of tests and awaiting clearance, he ran away. He was found at home. I spoke to him, and he agreed to go to treatment. Two months later, he returned and looked the best I had ever seen him. I was now simply just one of his doctors, his psychiatrist. He signed a five-year contract for monitoring by addiction medicine, AA, The Caduceus Group, and individual therapist.

Worsening

There are many more details, but the long and the short of it is that he didn't do well, even with all of this oversight and monitoring in place. Several months into recovery, with no evidence of any additional stress, his mood began to dip. Despite my increasing his medication, his suicidal urges returned. While walking home with a friend from an AA meeting, he threatened to jump off the bridge they were on. He went with this man to a nearby emergency room. Over the next year, two psychopharmacology colleagues of mine worked intensively with him, but he made little improvement. With his risk of suicide intensifying, I admitted him to the hospital where I worked. He improved only marginally with a full course of ECT. He wanted desperately to be home and we concluded that he was safe to be released. He was on many different medications and very sedated, and I spent the next several weeks slowly tapering him off some of these and stopping others. He was then able to attend and commit to an intensive psychotherapy program for treatment resistant depression.

At this point, Dr. Z had been my patient for about three-and-a-half years. He voiced that he was no longer hopeful that he would survive this. Always polite and deferential, he was non-committal and quiet when I tried to restore his optimism. It seemed as if my hopefulness – and that of the other professionals working with him – no longer worked for him. He was less forthcoming in our sessions and seemed to be slowly pulling away. Our visits felt stilted and he was mostly morose and gloomy. He began to miss visits, not only with me but with other members of the team. He confessed to what he termed "three half-assed suicide attempts" over the previous month. He swallowed a handful of one of his medications that he'd been hoarding, but this only made him sleep and feel groggy the next day. He tried inhaling household cleaners and bleach which at most made him feel nauseated. And he plotted about electrocuting himself in his bathtub while grasping the open socket of a lamp. He summed this up with a sad, self-demeaning sentence: "See how far I've sunk, that I can't do anything right anymore."

Normally a fastidiously dressed and handsome man, Dr. Z's appearance changed. He looked increasing disheveled, was often unshaven, and his face looked ruddy and swollen. I could smell alcohol and he didn't deny that he was drinking again. His sponsor urged him to go back to AA, which he did, though he refused the advice of his addictions counselor to return to rehab. He became increasingly irritable with his family members and people treating him. Because he came to two consecutive meetings of the Caduceus Group semi-intoxicated – and would not admit that he had been drinking, and then accused other members of ganging up on him – he was put on leave for two weeks. He also fired his addictions counselor for no valid reason. I attempted to meet him half way and found someone new for him to see. He did attend visits with her and stopped drinking for a while, but soon his monitoring broke down when he refused to give urine specimens.

His Final Week

Dr. Z missed a visit with me just before I was leaving for a five-day conference. I called him at home. He was apologetic and this seemed sincere. He had overslept. He actually sounded clear over the phone and told me that his mood was not bad. I made a note in his file that he sounded "sober." He agreed to meet with my office partner (who had seen him once before when I was on vacation) for a single visit while I was away. He kept that visit, denied having had a drink in about three weeks, and a suicide risk assessment was negative. My partner thought he looked "pretty good." I returned to the city two days later and was only home for an hour or so when I got a call from the hospital that Dr. Z was unconscious in the ER. He had been brought in by emergency medical services who were called by a neighbor of his. She heard a loud bang and looked outside, and to her horror, saw Dr. Z hanging from a bicycle hook on the deck of his apartment.

When I arrived at the hospital, Dr. Z was on a respirator, gravely ill. I spent time with the doctors and nurses who were tending to him. I tried to fill them in on the course of his illness and provide significant medical and psychiatric history. They seemed stunned that Dr. Z had tried to kill himself. My input helped them grasp the magnitude of his hopelessness and the long battle he waged with both depression and alcohol. When a doctor is a patient in an emergency room, there is always a certain amount of curiosity amongst the house staff. Throughout my career I've always been hospital based, and I've never been quite sure what this interest means, though I don't think it's prurient or sinister; rather, it's most probably rooted in the stereotypic and timeworn belief that doctors are immune from life's travails and diseases. And perhaps too, hospital personnel just want to make sure that a doctor-patient receives good care.

Dr. Z's parents were in a designated room off the emergency room for families and close friends of critically-ill patients. I had met them before, when Dr. Z was in the psychiatric unit, and again a couple of times in my office. We hugged each other for a comfortable while, and then I sat down opposite them. Such a sweet, lovely couple, in their seventies. His mother said: "I knew this was coming... but now that it has, I'm not quite ready..." His father, always a man of few words, was quiet and said nothing. He didn't need to. His face showed his grief and his dignified and composed posture reminded me that he was a veteran. He was sturdy and attentive to his wife. I can't remember much more, but it felt peaceful to sit quietly with them, and I was grateful for that time.

In consultation with Dr. Z's doctors, Mr. and Mrs. Z made the difficult decision to take their son off life support over the next thirty-six hours. They invited me to be present. Under my breath, I recited the Jewish prayer for a patient who has just died. The first sentence is *"Adonay natan, ve'Adonay lakah; yehi shem Adonay me'vorkakh. The Lord has given, the Lord has taken away, blessed be the name of the Lord."* Dr. Z looked very peaceful. The neurologist attending him was a classmate of his from medical school. I marveled at his composure, his gentleness and his kindness to all of us. The day before, the senior neurologist (whom I knew) and I, met with this young man and told him that it was perfectly acceptable to us if he excused himself from Dr. Z's care. He responded with: "Thank you, but no, I want to be his doctor. It means a lot to me to look after him, to give him something that he wasn't able to give himself." We were both speechless. And awed.

A Belated Home Visit

After Dr. Z was taken off life support, as we were saying our goodbyes, his sister mentioned that she was going to drive by his apartment to make sure that everything was safe and secured. No one had been there since EMS brought Dr. Z to the hospital. Adding that she felt a little nervous about doing this on her own, I asked if she'd like me to meet her there; she was relieved and that's what we did. When we walked in, I was struck by the condition of Dr. Z's home. Dirty dishes in the sink, empty food containers, overflowing garbage receptacles, an unmade bed, clothes and towels on the floor, and, most significantly, a number of empty bottles of Scotch whiskey. I now had a visual depiction of what happens to a bright and hardworking person overcome with crippling depression. Overwhelmingly sad. Sadness compounded by the fragments of rope attached to the bicycle hook on the deck, a reminder of the work of EMS cutting him down.

We didn't stay for long, but I realized that each of us was simultaneously searching for a suicide letter. His sister scanned the files on his computer, as I looked for handwritten evidence on his desk, kitchen counter and bedroom nightstand. We found nothing.

The Next Few Days

Dr. Z's mother called me the following day at my office to tell me that she woke up feeling guilty. Guilty? About what? That she had slept through the entire night without waking up. She thought that was odd, for a mother to lose her child, and then have an uninterrupted sleep. She wondered what I thought about that, but she answered her own question when she told me that this was the first time she had slept through the night in over a year. That she's never stopped worrying since Dr. Z's last suicide attempt. "But now I don't have to worry anymore. His suffering is over."

The next day, Mrs. Z called again. She wanted to give me the date and time of Dr. Z's memorial service. She hoped I could come and, if so, she asked if I could say a few words about him. I was stopped short. I demurred, and told her that I needed to give it thought. I mentioned my considerations about privacy and confidentiality, and then said that I would get back to her in a day or two. She reassured me not to feel pressured. Why she and her husband wanted me to speak was because "of how he died," and that as a psychiatrist I might be able to "educate the people coming to the service who don't understand." I've attended a number of funerals, memorials and wakes of my patients, including others who had died by suicide, but I had never been asked to speak in such a context before. On top of the grief that I was feeling about losing a patient whom I'd been treating for four years, this really felt ponderous.

Over the next day, I talked to a number of people about my dilemma. In addition to my wife and my office colleagues, I called friends and other psychiatrists, and most were clear in saying that I simply had to decline. That it would be inappropriate, ethically wrong and a breach of the doctor-patient covenant. I called my former therapist and was able to snag a one-hour cancellation. Masterful at what he does, he had me explore the massive cauldron of feelings I was having about this, and let me know that he was confident that at the end of the day I had to do what was right for me. When I left his office, I was still undecided, but I felt stronger and less conflicted about what that decision would be.

The Game-Changer

I returned to the hospital from my therapist's office, and as I was sorting through my inter-hospital mail I came upon a hand-written letter. I opened it up and read the following:

"Dear Dr. Myers,

Sorry, I just couldn't go on. I know you tried hard. But I lost faith that I'd get well again. Sorry. Please help my mom. Thanks for helping."

I felt my eyes filling up as I read – and re-read – Dr. Z's note, and it suddenly became clear to me that I would speak at his memorial service. I took his request literally - to help his mother. My willingness to do this would be one way of assisting each of them. I realized too, as I thought about his dispatch, that in the chaos and frenzy of his last moments of life, Dr. Z had devoted or preserved a few minutes to dash off these sentences, thanking me and thinking about his mother's well-being, even taking the time to post it. I now understood why family members who lose someone to suicide are obsessed with finding a note, and how disappointing it is for them to learn that most suicide victims do not leave one. And many who do are unable to craft a note that is clear or of solace. But Dr. Z's note was also a gift to me – and indirectly, to his mother. His words tempered my grief and gave me much consolation over the weeks and months ahead.

The Memorial Service

Dr. Z's memorial service was held at his parents' home. It was informal and warm, yet dignified and respectful. There were short eulogies before mine, delivered by a family member and a few friends. They all mentioned or alluded to the reality that Dr. Z had died by his own hand. No surprises here, no mystery, no elephant in the room. This made it much easier for me. I had already decided, with full agreement of Dr. Z's parents, not to openly disclose my relationship with him. They could do that for themselves, if they wondered. I was introduced simply as Dr. Myers.

I began by thanking Dr. Z's parents for asking me to say a few words. I highlighted and lauded their transparency, their honesty and courage in openly revealing that Dr. Z had died by suicide. I thanked the previous speakers as well for doing this. I added that their genuineness about how he died honored him and how he led his life, with openness and straightforwardness. I also told them that they were chipping away at the dangerous stigma that accompanies mental illness in our society. Here are a few statements that I made:

"All of you here who knew John well know that he lived with an awful illness. Clinical depression is a medical disorder. There are always psychological and social factors that play a part - and they did in John's case - but the major component is a biochemical deficiency in a specific

part of our brains. Depression is not a personality flaw, it is not a moral failing, it is not a weakness of will. And suicide is the only way out of the agony for some people. The last nine months of John's life were a horrific struggle for him. His heavy mood eclipsed many of his days. His death last week represents the end of a long, painful and tiring journey.

"Two weeks ago, while I was away at the American Psychiatric Association's annual meeting. I listened to a plenary address by William Styron. He has worked tirelessly to fight stigma in our society against those living with mental illness. Styron's book chronicling his own illness of depression is called Darkness Visible: A Memoir of Madness. *His book is one of the best, and most gripping, accounts of clinical depression - and its association with alcohol dependence. Styron spoke with passion and with humility, and one sentence from his moving address has particularly affected me. And I quote him: 'At my worst point, if given the choice, I would have undergone amputation of a limb without anesthesia, anything to make the hell go away.'"*

I made a few other statements and then closed by reading an old Korean poem, inspired by Buddhism, from the mid-8th century. It is called "Requiem for the Dead Sister" by Master Wolmyong (c. 742-765).

What isn't depicted here is how overcome by emotion I was as I made my remarks. Anticipating a certain amount of this, I strategically wrote out on paper everything I planned to say. And I rehearsed. In addition to the intensity of my relationship with Dr. Z, and its duration, there was something else. What I hadn't anticipated was that there would be so many people there whom I knew, or who knew me. Many of his classmates had been students of mine and a few had been – or currently were – patients of mine. As I looked out at them, with their tearful and ashen faces, and many so young, I longed for my professorial or therapist cloak, the one we use to contain and shield us in the face of strong feelings. I felt disarmed, exposed, naked. It took me a while to accept that. And even celebrate that, my humanness. That I was a psychiatrist who had just lost a cherished patient to suicide. That we hurt too. That it's okay to grieve.

A Gift from Mrs. Z

Several months after Dr. Z's death, I was contacted again by his mother. She had just published, in booklet form, a diary that chronicled a two-week canoe trip that Dr. Z had made with his aging dog Niska. This occurred seven years before he first came to see me. "Would I like a copy?' Mrs. Z asked. I of course answered in the affirmative, trying to mute my excitement. Suicide is – and perhaps always will be – a mystery to those left behind. We look for anything that might give us more information, any clue into the mind of the person who has made that wrenching decision to die. But my curiosity and search for answers goes back decades. I first felt it in medical school while studying pathology and we observed our first autopsy or postmortem examination. Then it was reinforced during my internship and internal medicine residency, when it was mandatory to attend the autopsies of all those patients who had died under our watch and whose family signed consent for the procedure.

I carried this mindset into my training in psychiatry, when I lost patients to suicide, and then into my practice and teaching years.

Although I am not formally trained in conducting psychological autopsies, I've incorporated facets of this process when trying to retrospectively piece together why my patient took his or her life. Meeting with bereaved families is one part of this. Not only do I hope to offer comfort, and to answer questions asked that don't violate privacy and confidentiality, but I hope to learn something from them as well.

A Journey of Rivers and Rain is the title of the book published by Dr. Z's mother. Its preface gives a short biographical sketch of Dr. Z's many talents and accomplishments. There is a further personal tribute from his friends expressing how greatly he will be missed. I learned so much about him, and wished that the details of his trip had come up in our many sessions together. He wrote: *"This trip is of particular significance to me now since it was the last canoe trip I made with Niska. She died at the age of 14 years in March of 1989, a year and half after we left the North."* I knew that the loss of his precious dog and the sudden death of his best friend in a motor vehicle accident were major events that he had experienced. Both of these losses played a critical role in his depression. But I lacked information and specifics. Dr. Z's depression was so weighty and big that it eclipsed the rich tapestry of his life. So much was inaccessible, and it was impossible for the two of us to get below the surface of his daily struggles with his world, his tendency to isolate and to push people away.

This, however, was a happy time in his life. Reading his prose and the descriptive detail of his geographical surroundings, the capricious weather, making meals, finding sandbars to set up evening camp, and his tender affection for Niska was so revealing. There are three color photos of Niska, two of her alone and one with him. Dr. Z looks handsome and fit, and although his facial expression is neutral, he certainly does not appear to be depressed. It was a face I had never seen before, even when he emerged for brief periods from the worst throes of his depression. And although most of the passages he has written were upbeat, or prosaic even, there were several that gave me pause:

"I seem to be unable to fully embrace the moment — always reaching back to the familiar past or dreaming of a happier future. There is some deep inner turmoil brewing inside me, an unfulfilled, restless spirit struggling to avoid the dark demons lurking in the shadows of unconsciousness."

And this:

"My thoughts and emotions seem to be in a state of confused turmoil at the moment. I think that I am going through one of my lonely spells. Not lonely for the companionship of friends, but a more profound loneliness — a kind of sadness for all the dreams that might have been but never were and a wistfulness for special magical moments from times past."

All hindsight of course, but how I wished that I had a copy of this diary to pull out in our sessions. I would love to hear his response to a question I'd pose to him like: "Dr. Z, tell me about the dark demons you've written about?" Or this question: "Can you say more about the wistfulness you've mentioned here?"

In the Afterword to the book, his mother wrote four brief paragraphs. This sentence, quoted here, is one I wish to share:

"*The longstanding depression persisted, interfering with his work until he finally had a complete breakdown, and, in May of 1997, he took his life, still suffering from the 'profound loneliness' in spite of all those who loved him.*"

The Suicide Data Bank Project

Six years after Dr. Z's death, I was alerted to a project initiated by the American Foundation for Suicide Prevention. AFSP was founded in 1987 and is based in New York City. Its goals are to educate the public about suicide prevention, advocate for public policies to advance their mission, and fund innovative research to save lives. What I read is that they were interested in collecting and analyzing information from therapists about their patients who had died by suicide while in treatment. I decided to sign on and complete the necessary paperwork, which was extensive. For this memoir, I opened my saved files from this time and it was interesting to read "Therapist's Reaction Questionnaire." It's been seventeen years since I looked at this. Here's a summary:

The first question was to describe my relationship with the patient. I wrote *"We had a professional relationship, although having stated that, I am aware of the unique issues when one physician treats another. I felt comfortable and confident about my boundaries with him. I was certainly fond of him and I think that this might have been rooted in his profound sense of loneliness and isolation. He suffered a lot and was rarely joyous. But his unhappiness was never oppressive. He never made me feel incompetent as his doctor. He bore his pain with great dignity."*

Of the list of emotional reactions, I said "yes" to shock and disbelief: *"only at first, even when you know that someone's at high risk, you still can't believe it when suicide happens;"* grief: *"I had waves of grief for several weeks afterwards. I had been his psychiatrist for four years. That's a significant period of time. You feel a loss when you have worked together so intimately so long;"* self-doubt: *"as always, I wondered if I should have attempted another type of combination or augmentation strategy of his medications for his severe mood disorder. But it was the alcohol use that put him at imminent risk of suicide;"* anger/frustration: *"my anger is a diffuse type of anger that we psychiatrists can't save more lives from suicide. And yet, when people suffer as much as Dr. Z did, I have great sympathy for their anguish, fortitude and need for escape;"* anxiety: *"I worried that his friends and colleagues might judge me as a 'bad doctor.' That I had missed the boat with their friend and colleague;"* shame or embarrassment: *"I lived with a sense of this because Dr. Z's death was so public in medical circles."*

Of the list of emotional reactions, I said "no" to guilt: *"in my heart, I believed that I and the other team members had done as much as we could do. I was worried about his drinking and saw this as dangerous but he wouldn't or couldn't stop – and he refused to return to residential treatment;"* fear of blame: *"his parents and his sister were very kind and grateful for the care I provided. They never made me feel that I should have forced him back into the hospital or that I had failed;"* "no" to fear of lawsuit; and the following: inadequacy; betrayal; relief; hopelessness; dreams/fantasies related to the suicide.

Responding to other questions, I recorded that I held a debriefing session with several of the staff who had looked after Dr. Z when he was an inpatient several months earlier. I found this helpful for my healing and it was good to share experiences with my fellow staff colleagues. I mentioned that I met with both of his parents and his sister on one occasion about two weeks after the memorial service. When asked if there were any things that I might have done differently to prevent his suicide, I wrote: *"I could have certified him against his wishes but I honestly feel that this would have provided only short-term protection. He dreaded the idea of returning to hospital. He might have eloped, as he had done once before, or tried suicide on the unit. I don't actually know if changing his medications would have helped."*

One final question was about what influence the suicide might have had on my treatment of psychiatric patients in general and suicidal patients in particular. I wrote: *"I continue to learn. I tend to be cautious — I have always tried to err on the side of overreacting to suicidal patients. I have become much more specialized in the management of suicidal physicians and their unique issues around stigma, denial of illness, and propensity to dual diagnoses of mood disorders and substance abuse/dependence."*

In my face-to-face day-long meeting with the AFSP team, I found it stimulating to review, explain and elaborate upon the clinical details, my treatment strategies over the years, my therapeutic relationship with Dr. Z, and my relationships with all of the other health professionals who were involved in his care. I came away with new insights that have served me well since that time in my professional life. And I was pleased to have contributed to this research project, aspects of which have been published.[1,2,3] I didn't realize that my experience with colleagues (which was collaborative, and I think healthy) after Dr. Z's death was not necessarily the norm until I read the following in a letter to the editor:[2]

"...we wish to make a point about the tone in which some of the comments were conveyed... Rather than judgment, colleagues who are willing to openly discuss treatment cases that have ended so tragically deserve our support in examining their responses to the patient and exploring strategies and interventions that might have made a difference."

Dr. Z's Death Not in Vain

In my professional career I have met countless survivors of suicide loss who want to get involved in some way to prevent the suicide of others. There's a refrain that goes like this: "If by telling my story, of losing my husband to suicide, I can save one person from killing themselves then I will be clear that my husband did not die in vain." I resonate with this sentiment and that is why I've invoked the death of Dr. Z and my treatment of him in various teaching formats.[4-9] It is my hope that the many people attending, mostly psychiatrists and other mental health professionals, come away with new insights and strategies to use in their own clinical work. That they will save lives. One of my learning objectives, required for all scientific presentations, is always this: To put a human face to the tragedy of suicide.

Postscript

In my conversation and email exchange with Dr. Z's sister, she told me that a few weeks after he died, when she was sorting through his belongings, she found several handwritten pages, hidden away, in her brother's antique desk. One page she has re-ferred to as his suicide letter. It is undated and reproduced here.

"Why do I constantly feel so much pain deep inside
Why do I feel so alone
Why does my entire life seem to be full of failures
Why do I feel rejected by my friends
Why do I find it so hard to make new friends
Why do I find myself suddenly crying for no apparent reason
Why do I find myself feeling more down and sad after talking to
friends
Why do I feel so unloved and unlovable
Why does my entire future feel so hopeless
Why do I fear each day when it arrives
Why do I feel the life force slowly ebbing from my body
Why do I have these impulsive urges to end this life of mine so
fraught with pain and misery
Why do I constantly crave the painless peacefulness of death
What was the intended purpose of my being a part of this world
I want to depart and leave it all behind — the pain is more than
I can bear
Oh God, please take me now, please take me now."

References

1. H. Hendin, J.T. Maltsberger, A.P. Haas, "A physician's suicide," *American Journal of Psychiatry* 160(12) (2003): 2094-2097.

2. Letters to the editor, "Dr. H. Hendin and his colleagues reply," *American Journal of Psychiatry* 161(12) (2004): 2330-2331.

3. H. Hendin, A.P. Haas, J.T. Maltsberger, B. Koestner, K. Szanto, "Problems in psychotherapy with suicidal patients," *American Journal of Psychiatry* 163(1)(2006): 67-72.

4. Michael F. Myers, "Death of a physician by suicide," Clinical case conference presenter, American Psychiatric Association Annual Meeting (New Orleans, LA. May 25, 2010)

5. Michael F. Myers, "Death of a physician by suicide: A case conference," Grand Rounds. Department of Psychiatry. SUNY Downstate Medical Center (Brooklyn, NY. February 2, 2011)

6.   Michael F. Myers, "Death of a physician by suicide: A case conference," Grand Rounds. Department of Psychiatry. Coney Island Hospital (Brooklyn, NY. March 28, 2011)

7.   Michael F. Myers, "Death of a physician by suicide: A case conference," Grand Rounds. Department of Psychiatry. Maimonides Hospital (Brooklyn, NY. April 11, 2011)

8.   Michael F. Myers, "Coping with the suicide death of a patient: A case conference," American Psychiatric Association Annual Meeting (San Francisco, May 19, 2013)

9.   Michael F. Myers, "Suicide by a patient: A case conference," American Psychiatric Association Annual Meeting (New York, NY, May 4, 2014)

Chapter Eight

Winding Down My Private Practice

"If you wanna fly, you got to give up the shit that weighs you down."

Toni Morrison, *Song of Solomon*. (New York: Knopf, 1977) 179.

As I approached my thirty-fifth year of clinical practice, I became increasingly pensive about next steps professionally. Should I continue what I'd been doing for so many years, half-time academic work and half-time private practice? I wasn't unhappy in either camp, but I wasn't filled with fervor either. My colleagues at work seemed to feel the same way, and even younger psychiatrists in our department talked about preparing for retirement. I felt restless, though this was offset by invitations to give lectures and present my work at various medical centers or national and international meetings. But there was also something else churning in me, something important and demanding of my attention. I needed to turn the lens on myself and look inward.

Getting Personal

I grew up feeling different, but it took time to recognize, pin-point and analyze my sense of otherness. In high school I felt like a hick, taking the long daily commute by bus from my family's farm in rural Chatham to attend Chatham Collegiate Institute, located in the urban center of our municipality. I was raised as a Roman Catholic, and although we were a sizable minority, I got my share of name-calling and teasing about meatless Fridays. I was academically precocious, skipped grades in my one-room country school and entered Grade 9 at age 11. I was physically smaller than my classmates, and not particularly gifted at sports, setting me apart in gym class. Not especially geeky or nerdy, I always had a few good friends which offset my loneliness. We all tended to be serious students and clearly college bound, not uncommon but not the norm either at my secondary school in the late 1950s. I spread my final year – Grade 13 – over two years, to give myself a chance to mature before heading off to university at age 17.

Over the next few years, my sense of feeling different crystal-lized. It was my sexuality. Although I started dating at a re-spectable age and almost always had a girlfriend, I was sexually repressed. I was a virgin for far too long and this embarrassed me deeply. Once I got into medical school, I immediately joined a fraternity and loved it – the sense of camaraderie, volunteer-ing for community events, meeting other guys who were not in medical school, becoming an officer, attending an international meeting, and most of all the parties. But I never discussed my sex life or, if pressed, I lied. I buried myself – that is, my libidinal self – in my medical studies, summer jobs, social life, hobbies and friendships.

Finding other men attractive didn't hit me until I was 23 years old. Unusually late. I was interning in Los Angeles and there was no mistaking that these feelings were real. I didn't act on them, and I told no one, including my fiancée at the time. I worked hard and played hard. Life was sweet, there was no turmoil, and I was happy. Even when I ended my engagement a year later, it was not about whether I thought I might be gay. But it was not long after that when I was approached by a man in a nondescript bar where the doctors and nurses hung out in downtown Detroit. It felt exciting and daring. The reality was quite the opposite when we slept together later that night. I'm not sure what I expected. This was my first one-night stand – and not my last. I went to work the next day and carried on with my life, continuing to pass as straight. It was a persona that I honed for decades.

Upon returning to Los Angeles, and over about three months, I frequented a few gay bars in Hollywood and went home with other men. Mostly, I found sex enjoyable and exciting. But, with the exception of one man, I never slept with anyone more than once. Nor did I want to. I didn't feel good afterwards.

This was the summer of 1968, an internally lonely time in my life. I had made good friends at the hospital and didn't lack for company and fun, but I told no one about my Hollywood forays. I was full of shame. Apart from the strangers I went home with, I knew absolutely no one who was gay. In fact, I had never even

heard of a gay doctor. I had learned from my medical education that homosexuality was a disease. A perversion. A sexual
deviation. Continuing on this path scared me. Could I remain
in medicine and be gay? The bars that I went to were dark and
seedy. Much like New York City in the late 1960s, there must
have been a more sophisticated, albeit underground, gay scene in
Los Angeles but it would have been lost on me. I never inquired
or attempted to explore it. Using my restricted and distorted
yardstick, I concluded that there didn't seem to be anything
"gay" about being gay. I went back into a closet that I'd never
left and slammed the door shut.

That fall I met my wife-to-be. I told her about my gayness on
our first date. To my surprise she didn't run for the hills. As our
relationship developed, I accepted myself as bisexual. We got
married in 1969. The short version is that we had a good run
of marital and family life for forty years. Ups and downs and
bumps along the way? - yes, but it was only the final five years
or so when my same-sex feelings returned – with intensity and
ascendancy. I came out as a gay man at the age of 64, arriving,
finally, at a place of accepting myself. I don't need to hide anymore. Or to blush or avert my eyes if someone questions my
sexual orientation.

As a gay doctor, I stand on the shoulders of giants in psychiatry.
One of them is Dr. John Fryer, who was instrumental in getting
the American Psychiatric Association to remove homosexuality
from its diagnostic nomenclature in 1973. He appeared masked
as "H. Anonymous, MD" at APA's 1972 annual meeting. "My
greatest loss is my honest humanity" he said. "How incredible

that we homosexual psychiatrists cannot be honest in a profession that calls itself compassionate and helping." It was twenty-two years later that Dr. Fryer revealed that he was the masked man on the APA panel. He had been forced to leave his psychiatry residency at the University of Pennsylvania when it was discovered that he was gay.[1]

And so, I come full circle. It is my otherness that fundamentally – but not with full awareness – attracted me to psychiatry, and ultimately to becoming a doctors' doctor. I've been able to empathize with my doctor patients burdened with the scourge of mental illness, coping with brokenness, and struggling for acceptance and belonging in a profession of perfection and stature. I understand what it's like to feel a bit of a misfit, less than, unclean and tattered. But as a wounded healer, I know the restorative value of listening, acceptance, caring, doggedness, and hope. I bask in the glory of doctors getting well again, plying their skills, serving their patients, comforting, and saving lives. What more could any man ask for?

Most, but not all, memoirists are people of a certain age – and I am one of them. I could not have written this book at an earlier time of my life and given it its due. I wasn't ready. Although this is my ninth book, it is the first one with the authenticity and honesty that a true memoir demands and a reader deserves. About two years ago, when I began to muse on this project, I became aware that I could not chronicle my journey of becoming a doctors' doctor without disclosing this essential piece of my own story, not just the stories of the doctors I was writing about. As the months passed and my internal dialectic resolved itself, I relegated my final vestiges of shame to the dustbin. I was now able to put pen to paper.

Retiring from Private Practice

My wife and I separated in August of 2007 and I took an apartment in downtown Vancouver. Over the next few months, and with the assistance of my therapist, I made the decision to close my private practice. The good news is that I had more than eight months to discuss this with my patients. My immediate concern was for those who had been in my care for many years. Most of these doctors were stable but would still need someone to take over the management of their medication. There is a massive shortage of psychiatrists, so I was fortunate that a handful of my colleagues kindly accepted one or two of my patients into each of their practices. Other patients of mine preferred to have their primary care physician oversee their medication. A common refrain was: "I don't want to start all over again with a new psychiatrist. My family doctor knows me pretty well. If, down the road, I have a set back or my medication stops working, then my doctor can refer me to a psychiatrist."

Retiring from practice is tough for all physicians. Saying farewell to patients whom you've known for a long time is never easy, but it's a fact of life. Both my patients and I agreed that it was a gift to be able to discuss the process over months, before the final visit. Many doctors and their patients do not have this luxury. Often, doctors become seriously ill quickly and have to stop seeing patients over a few short weeks. Some die suddenly with no goodbye. Others, for reasons beyond their control, may be terminated from their job, or relocate quickly for personal and family reasons. For psychiatric patients who've had the same psychiatrist for years, this kind of ending is crushing and may reactivate old wounds. They feel betrayed, abandoned, angry, adrift, sad. Over my career I have inherited patients in this situation. Most gradually made the transition to my care, but not always. Their grief at losing someone so cherished and idealized was too great for me to satisfy them.

I did not accept new patients into my practice, except for a few who were fine with being told over the phone that I was retiring in seven months, or five months, or whatever the timeline became. These doctors were acutely ill and needed medication and supportive psychotherapy. I felt confident that I would be able to help them in the short term, and once their immediate symptoms were gone, we could discuss next steps.

I was most concerned about my doctor-patients who were in active psychotherapy treatment, technically called long-term psychodynamic psychotherapy. Six or seven months was not enough time. One particular doctor, whom I remember clearly, in response to my retirement news said: "But I won't be finished by then." I totally agreed and told her that. I had been seeing her every two weeks for about three years. She was a model patient - reflective, organized, and prepared for each visit. She had made huge gains, especially in her self-esteem, after coming through a stressful divorce and recovering from adolescent sexual trauma and loss. We used our few remaining visits over the months with great efficiency and productivity. Note the language here - it's both deliberate and accurate. Like two physicians tackling a medical problem, we rolled up our sleeves and got to work making the best of our time together. We were of course two physicians, but doctor and patient, not work colleagues, not research collaborators, not a medical team in the operating room. Our final visit was eased by the knowledge that a dear colleague and friend agreed to take over and continue her psychotherapy. I knew that she was in good hands.

Falling from Grace

It did not take long for the news that my marriage had ended and my wife and I were living apart to spread through the medical community of Vancouver. I anticipated this. Even before separating, this was a theme in my discussions with my therapist. I worried that my reputation would suffer a fatal blow, that I would become the laughing stock of doctor colleagues and doctors who knew of me only through my profile, the "doctors' doctor." What kind of credibility would I have as a psychiatrist who treats doctors and whose own marriage had failed? Even more poignant, what about my image as a marital therapist to doctors? This hit home shortly after my separation, when one of my best friends, a fellow psychiatrist known for his sarcasm, and I were out for a walk on the beach. He said: "Let me recommend a couple of books to you - *Doctors' Marriages* and *Men and Divorce*" (my first two books, published, respectively, in 1988 and 1989). I laughed, but that was just a cover for how badly I felt inside.

What I did find helpful was talking to my associate Dr. Glen Gabbard, with whom I was then co-authoring a book. I told him about my separation and he was wonderful and extraordinarily kind. Not only was he spot-on in his empathy but he hit the bulls-eye with his advice. That yes, my doctor-patients will struggle with this news and question my ability to be helpful. But he urged me to keep in mind the phenomenon we call "idealized transference," where one's psychiatrist is viewed as all-knowing. That those already in treatment with me may lose their ballast, will feel uncertain or confused, and will test my ability and capacity to be present, strong and committed. He reminded me that others couldn't care less about my personal life, as long as it didn't disrupt what they expected from me.

I will never forget what happened the next day after talking to Glen. I was scheduled to see a two-doctor couple whom I had been seeing for several months. They sat down and she looked at him and said: "Do you want to tell him or should I?" He said: "No, I'll do it." They both looked and sounded so serious. I sat quietly but I was a mess inside. So insecure and full of doubts. What was coming? Sorry, this will be our last visit? He said: "We heard the news that you and your wife have separated. We talked. It's none of our business. We just want you to know that we hope you're okay. But, this does not take away from our sessions here. You have helped us so much. We hope we can keep seeing you. Is that possible?" I said: "Of course. Thank you for your concern. I'm doing okay... So, let's get to work. What's on the agenda for today?" And the visit unfolded. Their sweet words made my day!

I will never know of course if there were others who judged me by what was happening in my personal life. But that's fine. How individuals choose a psychiatrist is a complicated business, and even more so when two people in the midst of marital turmoil are discussing whom they'd like to see. The stakes are even higher when one or both are physicians themselves; understandably, they're going to do their homework in seeking out a colleague whom they think is best equipped to help them.

Relocating

In addition to closing my private practice, I also decided to make a whole new start. I accepted a new position, a full-time academic job, in New York City. My official title was Vice-Chair for Education and Director of Residency Training, Department of Psychiatry & Behavioral Sciences, SUNY Downstate Medical Center in Brooklyn. Although I would no longer have a private practice, I had no intention of abandoning my moniker of being a doctors' doctor. I wouldn't be directly treating medical students and physicians, but I'd continue to be involved by supervising psychiatry residents who were. In this way, I could still impart my knowledge and experience as a clinician to doctor-patients while continuing to stay current. Little did I know then, in 2008, that I was embarking upon a whole new phase of becoming a doctors' doctor.

References

1. A. Levin, "Courageous actions led to removal of homosexuality as a diagnosis in the American Psychiatric Association's Diagnostic and Statistical Manual," *Psychiatric News.* (October 15, 2019): psychnews.psychiatryonline.org

Chapter Nine

Fighting for Physician Wellness in the Pre-Retirement Years

"...never give in, never, never, never, never—in nothing, great or small, large or petty—never give in except to convictions of honor and good sense."

Winston Churchill, Harrow School, Harrow on the Hill, London, October 29, 1941

I started my new job in Brooklyn with verve – and a steep learning curve – on July 1, 2008. I wore two hats, distinct but with significant overlap. It was exciting to be the program director, taking the helm of responsibility for training SUNY Downstate resident physicians in psychiatry, forty-eight in number. My assistant, Dr. Ellen Berkowitz, was a godsend. She helped me with the nuts and bolts of issues specific to this country, insofar as they were different from my professional experiences in Canada. My second charge, Vice-Chair of Education, gave me a broader swath of teaching endeavors in the entire department.

This meant that the directors of medical student education and the fellowship directors (child and adolescent psychiatry, and geriatric psychiatry) all reported to me. And I represented our department on a number of Dean's committees and ad hoc meetings with the other medical schools in New York City.

Coming Home, Sort Of

Having spent two formative years of my postgraduate medical training at Los Angeles County General Hospital in the 1960s, it was both exciting and somewhat nostalgic to now work at Kings County Hospital Center, which is affiliated with SUNY Downstate and owned by NYC Health + Hospitals, the municipal agency that operates all of New York City's public hospitals. Located directly across Clarkson Avenue from SUNY Downstate Medical Center, the first time I came up to street level from the Winthrop Street subway station and saw KCHC in the near distance, my face lit up. And I felt a warmth in my chest. Although architecturally different than Los Angeles County General, they are both imposing, yet welcoming, structures. Welcoming because both institutions have always provided care for the medically underserved, uninsured, and racial and ethnic minority citizens. The inscription over the front door of LACGH reads: "The doctors of the attending staff give their services without charge in order that no citizens of the county shall be deprived of health or life for lack of such care and services."

But there was another reason why I had a soft spot in my heart for Downstate. A large number of their medical graduates headed out west in the mid- to late-1960s for their internships, and I met several of them in 1966 at LACGH. Having trained in Canada, I didn't have as much hands-on experience at they did, and they taught me how to perform many basic medical and surgical procedures that I had previously only observed at my medical school and its teaching hospitals. They had a comfort level with the patients, mostly Hispanic and African American, because they had learned from their ethnic equivalents at KCHC. And some were quintessential New Yorkers - they talked fast, were outspoken, friendly, and fun – and they made a huge impression on me.

Becoming the Ombudsman for Medical Students

Minus a private practice, my workdays now were a major departure from my professional life in Canada. And yet, the notion in my mind of physician health and wellbeing never disappeared— in fact, it didn't even make it to the back burner! Within weeks of arriving, our Dean at the time, Dr. Ian Taylor, created a new position, ombudsman for the medical students, and asked me to take this on. Dean Taylor and I shared the same ethos, that the health of our students was precious and must be safeguarded in their four years with us. My task was to evaluate and resolve any complaints that medical students had about being mistreated in the course of their education.

Mistreatment, either intentional or unintentional, occurs when behavior shows disrespect for the dignity of others and unreasonably interferes with the learning process. Broadly defined, this might include being berated or humiliated by a professor or resident teacher; being asked to perform personal errands while missing teaching activities; or being harassed because of one's race, gender, ethnicity, religion, sexual orientation or gender identity. Mistreatment causes anxiety and can be destabilizing and demoralizing in many students.

Beyond dealing with each individual complaint, I have heeded Benjamin Franklin's maxim "An ounce of prevention is worth a pound of cure." I learned quickly that the perpetrators of medical student mistreatment were not bad people, rather most were simply out of step with what is deemed acceptable or professional in today's medical academy. I decided to meet with each department to explain my role in the medical school. Certain older professors have struggled with purging their sexist language and mannerisms, and a number of international medical graduates have had to adapt to a teaching context that is different than that of their country of origin, where they came of age in medicine. Certain physicians, especially surgeons and surgical subspecialists, have needed to learn that bullying and shaming techniques are not acceptable today, though they may attempt to defend their actions with the timeworn excuse that this is how they were trained.

To drive home my point, I have repeatedly shared a disguised case from my private practice. It's a compelling story and one that invariably captures the attention of even the most cynical doctors in the audience. Here it is:

Dr. Gin was a third-year resident in general surgery. He came to see me six weeks after he began to slip into a clinical depression. He described his mood as flat and dull, he had lost about seven pounds of weight, he was having trouble concentrating, he was waking up very early in the morning, and his self-confidence had gone into free fall. He wasn't struggling with hopelessness or thoughts of suicide. Because he had lived through a similar bout in medical school, and had received treatment, he knew what was wrong. I started him on the same antidepressant that had worked for him before and scheduled a return visit with him in a week.

The night before that appointment I got a call from his partner, Dr. Rand, who was also a resident. He was in a panic. Dr. Rand had come home from work, startled to find Dr. Gin standing on the balcony of their 21ˢᵗ-floor apartment. It was dark, the middle of winter, and Dr. Gin seemed to be in a sort of "dazed, altered state." He grabbed hold of him and coaxed him back inside, locked the sliding door, and made sure he was safe. They talked for a few minutes and that seemed to help. Dr. Gin calmed down, they ate a light dinner, but, still worried, Dr. Rand phoned me. I made a house call.

When I asked Dr. Gin about being out on the balcony, he said: "I was debating whether to jump or not." He sighed, took a deep breath, and another, and added: "Thank god for Alex, coming home when he did, I'm not sure what might have happened. I'm okay now, that was scary." I expressed my relief too, and asked him what might have led up to this. Here's what I learned.

"We were making afternoon rounds with my team. I wasn't at my best, I was tired, I had been up all night in the operating room. My attending physician started grilling me at the bedside of one of my patients. I was trying to explain her test results but I guess I wasn't doing it right, or fast enough, he kept interrupting me and asking me questions as if this was an exam. I could feel myself getting more and more anxious, getting things

wrong, contradicting myself and then he just blew up 'Gin, what's your problem? This is a pathetic performance. How'd you get this far in your training? I won't embarrass you by asking one of the medical students to answer my questions, questions that any medical student could ace.' He kept going on and on, seemed like an eternity. No one said a word. I think they were stunned. You know what happened? My patient spoke up and said to him 'Doctor Ames, forgive me for butting in, but aren't you being a little hard on my doctor?' He stopped. Nothing more was said. We finished the rounds. He left. Two of the other residents talked to me and that helped. I walked home. But I kept thinking about what happened. As pissed as I was at Dr. Ames, I thought he was right, that I did do a horrible job at presenting my patient to him, that it was inadequate, and inferior. I let myself down, I let my patient down, I let my team down. I began to doubt if I had what it takes to be a good doctor, a capable surgeon, the balls to be tough, not show any weakness. Next thing I knew, I was on the balcony."

I re-assessed Dr. Gin and concluded that he was safe at home. This came as a relief to him and Dr. Rand. He did not want to be hospitalized. We all agreed that he needed a good night's sleep. I saw him the next day in my office, and he felt much better, but I put him on medical leave. He needed more time for the antidepressant medication to start working. In two weeks, he was almost back to baseline and he returned to work.

I strongly believe that Dr. Gin could have killed himself. Dr. Rand's coming home when he did was fortuitous, and quite possibly saved his life. My message to attending physicians is blunt: teaching by shaming is unprofessional, never acceptable, and can be dangerous. Even if you were trained this way, and obviously survived it, does not make it right. Your trainees may be battling with depression, or others illnesses, and *although not 100 percent, they're still able to work and function effectively. Abusive teaching is enough to push them over the edge.*

At the end of the day, my educational meetings with the doctors in the various branches of medicine at our medical school have been well received. Medical student complaints about mistreatment have fallen each year. I continue in this position to this day.

Supervising Others Who Treat Medical Students and Physicians

Although retired from my private practice of treating doctors, I've had two other opportunities at our medical center to provide service and keep my hand in helping fellow physicians. The first has been my having monthly meetings with the clinical psychologists who treat our health sciences students at the Student Counseling Center. Although they each hold a PhD degree and work autonomously, they welcome the opportunity to meet with a senior clinician who has my unique experience in physician health. Our sessions enable them to discuss cases with me of individuals who are a bit more complicated and challenging. And because I'm a psychiatrist and they're all psychologists, I am able to add a medical perspective to their understanding when that's relevant. Together we decide if their patient might benefit from medication, and I can support a referral to one of our staff psychiatrists available to consult on medical student patients.

The second has been providing psychiatric supervision to our senior residents in psychiatry who treat medical students in our ambulatory psychotherapy clinic. Beyond the usual principles of psychotherapy that define faculty supervision of trainees in psychiatry, I have been able to offer something distinctive with respect to the intricacies of psychotherapy when both therapist and patient are physicians, albeit the latter still a student.

Here is an example that illustrates what I mean:

Dr. Elliott, a fourth-year resident, had been treating a third-year medical student for about six months, when I became her supervisor. Ms. James had been referred to the clinic after her boyfriend, a classmate, suddenly ended their two-year relationship. Not only was she grieving the loss of her boyfriend but her loss was complicated by the fact that her "ex" was now dating another woman in their class. She and Dr. Elliott had been meeting weekly for psychotherapy and all was going well. Not only was Ms. James now beginning to heal and regain her self-esteem, but she was looking at her history of unsatisfactory — and unhealthy — previous relationships with men. When I began to supervise Dr. Elliott, Ms. James had started her fourth year and began to miss a number of appointments because of the demands of her clinical rotations. Dr. Elliott was accepting and understanding, explaining that this is what it's like when you're a busy medical student, your work encroaches on your personal time and you're at the mercy of training expectations and schedules.

In our supervisory sessions, I asked Dr. Elliott to think about this. Could there be anything below the surface that also accounted for Ms. James missing so many sessions? She queried whether I was suggesting resistance, that perhaps it had become too painful for Ms. James to engage in probing and unearthing old memories, conflicts, hurts and embarrassments of earlier relationships with boyfriends. I agreed, but also asked her to consider the phenomenon of self-sacrifice and masochism in doctors, that the profession in many ways demands selflessness and denial of one's one human needs. This not only led to Dr. Elliott exploring this with her patient but also to reflect upon her own thoughts and behaviors. Dr. Elliott admitted to me that she tended to do this herself, putting off matters that she thought were selfish and letting the demands of psychiatry residency eclipse her life. Armed with this new insight and orientation to her psychotherapy with Ms. James, Dr. Elliott was able to help her still meet the requirements of clinical services but not sacrifice her personal psychotherapy. With flexibility and paying attention on both their parts, they resumed a weekly schedule.

A Special Invitation

Toward the end of 2008, I got a telephone call inviting me to give the closing keynote address at the annual meeting of the Federation of State Physician Health Programs in New Orleans in April of 2009. I was delighted. I called my lecture "Broken Physicians: Reflections on Loss, Shame, Suicide and Healing." As is my way, I envisioned this as another chance to give voice to the courageous struggles of doctors with psychiatric illness. Stigma paralyzes them and they're reduced to suffering in silence. For decades, I've chosen to be their mouthpiece and chronicler. Here is a summary of the lecture:

I began with a disguised patient from my practice. In fact, the title of the lecture was sparked by the first few words that were uttered by this doctor when he came to see me: "I'm broken, Dr. Myers." I have written about this man in detail elsewhere, especially his actual and metaphoric sense of himself, what contributed to his brokenness, and how I treated him.[1] I went on to describe loss, so common in physicians who are unwell and in need of care.

This young doctor says it with raw eloquence.

"Dr. B was a 29-year-old resident who I treated in hospital for an acute psychotic episode. On morning rounds, he told my resident and me what it was like just after being admitted to the unit. 'All my clothes and possessions were locked up and I was placed on 1:1 observation. I was in the shower telling my nurse that I wanted to wash my hair. He was helpful and kind to me. But I paused in thought. Here I was standing there naked, thinking about all those years of study and hard work in medical school, for this. I had lost my career, my freedom, my privacy. My life had been reduced to a single dollop of shampoo.'"

I continued with this:

"Many physicians suffer from what I call aggregate loss. We grow up no strangers to loss. Loss of a parent by death. Loss of the family unit when our parents divorced. Loss of a father's presence because of his long hours of work. And because most of us are wounded healers, our backgrounds are riddled with loss. When I think of the plurality of doctors in the United States, and if I speak for us as a collective of physicians, we have survived poverty, hunger, war, forced migration, torture, family heartache, marital demise, alcoholism, suicide deaths of loved ones, physical/emotional/ sexual abuse, racial and ethnic discrimination, religious persecution, gay bashing, life-threatening disease, and other traumas and losses too numerous to count.

"But it is the rare physician who speaks openly and insightfully about the role of loss in their sense of collapse. Loss is a taboo topic in the house of medicine. The culture of medical training and medical practice selects for and rewards toughness and endurance. Loss and loser are only a column apart in the dictionary. Think about it. A third-year medical student learns that her mother's breast cancer has metastasized. The student may or may not take time away to be with her. At death, the student leaves immediately and spends roughly a week at home for the funeral and its aftermath. She returns to classes and clinics and is immediately immersed in catching up and responsibilities. Is this enough time to grieve? What does she do with her anger, sorrow, longing and heartache? It's no wonder that all of us who work in physician health see a new cluster of doctor patients each year who come at the end of residency. They all have the same goal — to give ascendancy to their own overdue needs and to examine unresolved or truncated loss."

I implored the doctors in the audience:

"Loss is ubiquitous in physicians. Look for it in your doctor patients who express their distress with physical symptoms. Look for it in your doctor patients with symptomatic drinking and drug dependency. Look for loss in physicians impaired by mood and anxiety disorders. Look for loss in physicians felled by a malpractice suit or licensure investigation. Those of you in positions of medical leadership, look for loss in the disruptive physician who comes to your attention in your work setting. And look for it in marital woes."

I want to share one final piece of this lecture, because although it occurred in 2009, I received an update last year, ten years later. This is a story from the portion of my address on physician suicide, where I read excerpts from an article written by my friend Dr. Beth Baxter. Beth is a psychiatrist in Nashville who lives with schizoaffective and bipolar disorder.

"My psychiatry residency training was rich in professional clinical experiences and dotted with personal experiences of severe clinical depression that grew closer and closer together in time, until they finally coalesced. In November of 1994, I made a suicide attempt that changed the course of my life.

"This attempt was my 'lowest ebb.' Knowing that things would have to change dramatically, I began to make the difficult steps toward learning to take care of myself. I grew in strength daily with the knowledge that my life had been spared. I asked myself how and why had I survived. The question of 'how' led me to a spiritual understanding of a loving and forgiving God. The question of 'why' was answered as I learned to love myself and to believe that my work on earth was not done. Through rigorous introspection, I learned to strip off my masks of 'doctor' and 'patient,' leaving my core features. I was finally able to feel whole without these masks.

"Beth told me she wrote this article so we, her colleagues in the health professions, could see that we too are human, and that serious mental illness knows no boundaries. Since that awful night in 1994, Beth has done well, which she credits to three factors: Clozapine, a kind and compassionate psychiatrist, and her faith.

"I have treated and interviewed many physician survivors of serious and near-lethal attempts at suicide. Many of them are religious – or certainly

acknowledge spirituality. The telephone call from Beth's therapist that interrupted her suicide attempt has meaning to her. Some form of divine act. That my time is not up yet. That my work as a physician is a gift from God, that he or she has spared me and wants me to keep living, and that I can help others."[2]

Last December we received a Christmas letter from Dr. Baxter. I have her permission to reproduce it here:

"On November 2nd of this year, I celebrated the 25th anniversary of my suicide attempt. Since that time, I have had many happy life events, and there have been more chapters of my personal history. However, the event of my suicide attempt continues to be one of the most important events of my life. It is by the grace of God that I survived it. But its other significance lies in the fact that it was the bottom of a long period of hard times for me. My life has been progressively much better since then.

Because you are receiving this letter, you have played a role in my recovery, and I am grateful for the support that you have given me. Your support has been in many different ways. You may be unaware of my suicide attempt, but you are probably aware of the struggle over the years that I have had with mental illness. You may also be unaware that your support has been that significant, but it was, and is. I am grateful for you.

I hope that you have a wonderful and joyous Christmas season. Maybe you can tell someone in your life how grateful you are for him or her. Gratitude is one of the most important gifts that we can give, and it is a gift to ourselves also. Strengthening our ability to have and show gratitude makes our lives happier and more meaningful.

Merry Christmas!

Beth"

Remembering Doctors Who Have Died by Suicide

On September 30, 2009, I delivered the Jeffrey Greenbaum Memorial Lecture at Zucker Hillside Hospital in Queens, New York. Dr. Greenbaum was a psychiatrist and a beloved teacher who took his life on August 20, 1991. I called my talk "Physician Suicide: New Findings." My approach when giving memorial lectures is to try and meld science with humanity. This enables the audience, especially the physicians, to learn and advance their knowledge on the subject, but also to be moved emotionally. I want to reach both their minds and hearts.

My lecture was eighteen years after Dr. Greenbaum's death. Although marking a sad event, I wanted to strike a chord of hope. I highlighted what we've learned in the interim about vulnerabilities in physicians and what we can do to intervene and save a physician's life. This was bookmarked by my opening and concluding slides. I started with these three slides:

1. "Every death leaves a conversation unfinished." Brent Staples, "John Hope Franklin," *New York Times* Editorial, March 27, 2009

2. "No one who has not been there can comprehend the suffering leading up to suicide, nor can they really understand the suffering of those left behind in the wake

of suicide." Kay Redfield Jamison, PhD. Forward to Michael F Myers and Carla Fine, *Touched by Suicide: Hope and Healing After Loss* (New York: Avery Publishing/ Penguin Random House, 2006) xiii.

3. "A photograph is a fragment – a glimpse......All photographs aspire to the condition of being memorable – that is, unforgettable." Susan Sontag, *At the Same Time: Essays and Speeches*. (New York: Farrar Straus Giroux, 2007) 126.

And I ended with this slide:

"Memories, even painful memories, are all we have. In fact, they are the only thing we are. So we must take very good care of them."

Elie Wiesel, quoted in Nina Beth Cardin, *The Tapestry of Jewish Time: A Spiritual Guide to Holidays and Life-Cycle Events*. (Springfield NJ: Behrman House, 2000) 16.

The year before, I had traveled to Winnipeg, Manitoba to give the Matthew Cohen Memorial Lecture on May 27, 2008. Dr. Cohen was an anesthesiologist at the University of Manitoba Medical School. He took his life January 16, 2007 and his colleagues and family were actively grieving. I called my talk "Medical Colleagues in Trouble: Recognizing Their Distress and Reaching Out." I was relieved that the atmosphere was less formal, giving me an opportunity before my lecture to meet many of his friends and colleagues and learn more about him. I am always interested in knowing how doctors have lived, not just how they died. I tried my best to convey the mystery of suicide, that despite all we understand, which is limited and imperfect, people we know will die by their own hand.

Fast forward in time to February 3, 2012, a day I spent in upstate New York meeting with physicians and other health professionals. They had lost a much-loved doctor "unexpectedly" a few weeks earlier. Everyone knew the cause of death but it was not publicly revealed. No matter. I am used to – and fully appreciate – the secrecy and privacy that accompanies suicide, given its pre-modern historical antecedents of crime and sin. Most important was that I was able to meet with many different groups of physicians, nurses, medical students, residents and other health professionals to talk about health, mental illness and suicide. I think they appreciated an outsider, who did not personally know the deceased, parachuting in to offer information on this tough subject. I was able to bring them together and create a safe place for them to ask questions and talk, reminisce and grieve in communion. As I traveled back to New York City that evening I had a great sense of gratitude and fulfillment. What gave me pause though is knowing that there are far too many medical communities who do not come together when they lose one of their own to suicide. They suffer alone, and often in silence.

As of this writing, I've given two other memorial lectures—the Vincent Uybarreta Memorial Lecture in 2010, and the Ben Shaffer Memorial Lecture in 2019.

Dr. Uybarreta was a first-year resident in surgery at SUNY Downstate Health Sciences University. He took his life August 25, 1998. He was only 25 years old. The Department of Surgery hosts a grand rounds every year or two in his name. Members of his family attend and one of them says a few words to introduce Vincent to the audience. They are warm, gracious people, and their presence has a noticeable impact, especially on the medical students and residents. The event enables everyone to take pause for an hour from their demanding schedules to remember, reflect, and pay attention to their wellbeing – and to watch out for each other.

Dr. Shaffer was a prominent and universally loved orthopedic surgeon and sports medicine physician in Washington, DC. He took his life May 20, 2015. His mother, and his sister Susan Solovay, have been tireless and steadfast in their determination that Ben will not have died in vain, and they are committed to advancing the treatment of mentally ill physicians. Ms. Solovay kindly volunteered to speak at a panel that I assembled at the annual meeting of the American Psychiatric Association in 2018. I called it "When Physicians Die by Suicide: Insights from Their Survivors."[3]

International Conferences on Physician Health

In the early 1990s, the Canadian and American Medical Associations began co-hosting a scientific conference, inviting individuals and groups invested in the health of physicians to come together in a shared learning environment. The meetings attract members of medical licensing boards, physician health programs, deans of medical colleges, academic researchers, leaders of medical associations, substance use treatment centers, and clinicians who treat physicians and their families. These sessions span three days and are held biennially. The British Medical Association joined the collaboration in 2008, so the meetings are now triple sponsored, rotating every two years around their respective countries. I've served on the planning committee a number of times since their inception.

Having attended quite a few of these meetings over the years, I've asked myself on many occasions - have these meetings helped me become a doctors' doctor; a better doctors' doctor; a better teacher of the science of physician health; a better scholar and contributor to the field? I don't fully know the answers to these questions, but let me list several thoughts, memories, and insights:

- I have the opportunity to submit a scientific abstract and enter the competition to have my work accepted for presentation. When my submission has been accepted and I present my work, it's gratifying to disseminate it and engage in discussion with those attending. When it's not accepted, I learn from sitting in on the sessions led by like-minded colleagues.

- I have met an extraordinary number of clinicians, researchers and administrators from all over the world who I've now joined in collaborative efforts. I'm convinced that this pluralistic endeavor advances physician health globally.

- I have listened to a number of outstanding keynote lectures. Their words have stimulated me, inspired me, touched me deeply, humbled me. Here's a sampling. Pediatrician Dr. Mark Vonnegut, author of *The Eden Express: A Memoir of Insanity*,[4] describing his psychosis in the 1970s, misdiagnosed as schizophrenia, then correctly as bipolar disorder. Neurosurgeon Dr. Frances Conley, author of *Walking Out on the Boys*,[5] chronicling years of humiliating sexual harassment at Stanford University Medical School before going public and shining a spotlight on this sexist scourge in American medicine. Surgeon Dr. Sherwin Nuland, author of *How We Die: Reflections on Life's Final Chapter*,[6] and many other books, recounting his paralyzing depression, hospitalization, and electroconvulsive treatments during his residency. Ms. Carla Fine, author of *No Time to Say Goodbye: Surviving the Suicide of a Loved One*,[7] telling the audience how she found her urologist husband Dr. Harry Reiss in his office, on his examining table, after he had killed himself, and sharing her long journey of healing.

- I have attended sessions that help me think outside the box. I've sat in on medical license officials arguing archaically why they request detailed psychiatric histories on their applicants. Or attorneys explaining the long winding course of malpractice litigation. Or presentations by medical students and residents about disclosing previous psychiatric treatment on their training applications. Or physician health programs debating the pros and cons of inpatient residential treatment for chemical and non-chemical addictions.

• I have come to know psychiatrists and psychologists in the trenches of physician health who, like me, have treated scores of physicians over the years. We speak a common language and know the challenges, the joys and heartaches of this kind of clinical work. A handful of them have been available to me when I've needed to consult with someone who can help with my treatment of a particular physician-patient that is not going well. Their availability, experience and honesty have assisted me greatly.

My presentations at the most recent international conferences - London in 2014, Boston in 2016, Toronto in 2018, and London again next year - are about the aftermath of physician suicide. In 2014, I shared my experiences in facilitating bereavement groups for physicians and other health professionals when they lose one of their own to suicide. This is especially important in small medical communities and in rural areas. Because everyone knows each other, the loss is far-reaching and painful, akin to losing a member of one's family. Grief can be complicated by the fact that if the doctor has been in active practice at the time of their death, many patients are left behind and the remaining doctors, often already in short supply and overworked, have to absorb these abandoned patients. The physicians may be angry, at times furious, at the doctor for killing themself, a confusing and guilt-producing emotion. Let me explain with an example:

I was about thirty minutes into facilitating a group of twenty-five primary care doctors who had come together in the hospital lounge. We were all seated in a horseshoe formation. They had lost a much-loved colleague six weeks earlier to suicide. Several physicians had spoken and mentioned many times over what a fine doctor he was and such a good man. He was revered by his patients and by the community for his leadership and volunteerism. Some doctors expressed regret that they knew he was struggling - he was going through a divorce - and that they didn't do more. They wished they had reached out and now it's too late. A few doctors were crying freely and quietly. The mood was sad and reflective, yet there was a discernably collective tone. Suddenly a doctor sitting alone at the back, who arrived a few minutes late and declined my invitation to join the formation, stood up and shouted: "This is so fucked up. We're sitting around like a bunch of idiots flagellating ourselves. I'm so pissed I could scream. He's the fucker who put a bullet in his brain - not us - we didn't murder him folks! He killed himself. We're the victims here, not him. And we're stuck with all his patients. Men, women and children who he just upped and abandoned. I don't know about you guys but I'm already burning out with my practice. We're all overworked and can't find more doctors to move here." At this point, he looked up toward the ceiling and shouted out: "Jim, you're a selfish asshole. I hope you're happy." He sat down. Understandably, there was an awkward silence. Just as I was about to comment, the doctor began to sob, quietly at first, then more loudly. One of the physicians walked over to him, sat down. and held him in her arms.

My presentations since 2016 have given me an opportunity to share my narrative research on physician suicide that I started in 2015. This was sparked by my belief that despite a range of scientific findings on physician suicide, there was a gaping hole:

information from the intimate others of doctors who had taken their own lives. The published literature is replete with studies of the personality and character traits of physicians, their psychological vulnerabilities, the psychiatric illnesses preceding their deaths, and the myriad stressors in their professional and personal lives. I wanted to capture the voices of people who knew doctors that had died by suicide, in the belief that they had observations, thoughts, hunches, theories of why this had happened.

So, in January of 2015, I began interviewing the family members, medical and nursing colleagues, classmates and roommates, training directors of residents, clerkship directors of medical students, and therapists of physicians and medical students who took their lives. After several months, I added two other groups of individuals whom I thought could assist with information: patients who lost their doctor to suicide, and physicians who had made serious suicide attempts but did not die. The interview format that I use is invitational, semi-structured, and comprehensive. I strive to make sure that those whom I'm interviewing have an opportunity "to tell their story." That's my guiding principle. Many have been conducted in person, but most have been done over the telephone or by Skype. Everyone is given a release form to sign after the interview, enabling me to use anecdotal information in my lectures, podcasts, scientific articles and books.

A word about the gestalt of the interviews. I respect the context, and remain keenly aware that I'm entering the world of individuals who are in the midst of grieving and healing, and that even with their permission or consent I may be disrupting a tenuous equilibrium. The persons themselves may not realize how fragile their current state is, that my asking certain questions can take them to a place that is full of sorrow or tension as recollections of their loved ones surface. This applies also to those whose loss was years or decades earlier. Being a seasoned psychiatrist helps me to sense or feel a nuance, a change in the person's speech or thought that is a warning, an alert, to heed. These encounters require great care, sensitivity, compassion, and always, humility. I'm constantly hoping that both of us will learn something new about their loved one's struggle, and take a degree of comfort from their process with me.

As of this writing, the number of interviews I've done is eighty-two, and the number of physician and medical student suicide deaths that these interviews arise from is fifty-one. These are physicians who lived and practiced in the United States, Canada, England and Australia. Here are a number of my key findings:

- Many of the individuals I interviewed, especially the spouses, parents, and children of doctors who died, were concerned about the demands of medical training and medical work on their loved one - they described this as taking a heavy toll on the overall health and functioning of the physician. This weight was compounded by additional personal and family stresses, like physical illness (diabetes, heart disease) or recent marital separation or divorce. They used terms like "burnout," "seemed more and more depressed," "trouble sleeping," "drinking more than usual," "obsessed with never feeling caught up," "gradually withdrawing from me and the family."

• Almost 15 percent of the doctors died without receiving any help. They did not or would not go to a primary care physician, psychiatrist, psychologist, counselor, or spiritual leader.

• Many of the doctors who did go for treatment felt deeply embarrassed and, not uncommonly, failed to follow the treating physician's orders, skipped appointments, or did not take the medication prescribed. Others preferred to prescribe their own medications.

• A number of the individuals I interviewed felt that their loved one was under-diagnosed, that he was more forlorn and possibly suicidal than was recognized. They weren't confident that their loved one was being honest with the treating health professional, fearing being hospitalized or reported to the medical licensing board. A few have felt that there needs to be more education and advanced training for health professionals who treat physicians.

• Family members often felt excluded from their loved one's care. They were not invited in to give their observations or to voice their worries. Too often their calls to the treating professional's office were not returned.

- After they lost their family member to suicide, some expressed feeling abandoned by their medical colleagues and other work associates. Doctors who survived a suicide attempt had similar feelings of being marginalized or shunned by their peers.

- The arc of impact after physician suicide is bigger than commonly believed, extending beyond family, to peers and classmates, to deans, designated institutional officials, and employers.

- Everyone I've interviewed has decried the stigma that is impeding ill physicians from receiving lifesaving treatment.

- All are committed to help prevent suicide in physicians in different ways, educating themselves about wellness, learning how to recognize worrisome behaviors in others and reaching out, attending and/or hosting grand rounds or other educational events, writing blogs, posting on social media, conducting research, publishing articles, volunteering at conferences on the aftermath of suicide.

I believe that these observations are particularly relevant for making change in our efforts to prevent suicide in physicians. Individuals whose lives have been touched by physician suicide are crafting a vision for humanity in medicine. They want those whom they've lost to be remembered, and they are insisting that new learning arises from their deaths. Many are also fighting stigma with courageous personal self-disclosure of their own stories of mental illness.

Independent Medical Examinations

Another way that I've kept active in physician health is by performing independent medical examinations (IME) on doctors who have been referred to the Committee for Physician Health (CPH) of the Medical Society of the State of New York. CPH provides non-disciplinary, confidential assistance to physicians, residents, medical students, and physician's assistants experiencing problems from stress and difficult adjustment, emotional, substance abuse and other psychiatric disorders, including psychiatric problems that may arise as a result of medical illness.[8] When a physician is referred to CPH by a colleague, employer or training director and speaks to one of the case managers, often the initial step is for the physician to undergo a comprehensive evaluation, an IME, to determine what's going on, be given a diagnosis (if there is one), and be appraised of treatment recommendations.

What follows is a sampling of situations that might prompt a referral to CPH:

- A final-year medical student, doing an elective in emergency medicine, has been consistently late for the beginning of her shift. When confronted, she blames the notoriously delayed subway trains. But she's also been found to be "missing in action" three times while on duty, not responding to her pager or cell phone, and her reasons are flimsy. Her site director has also found that compared to her first day on the job three weeks earlier, her interest and performance have dropped, which is highly unusual. When he met with her, she denied substance use, and when she reported to Employee Health she refused to give a urine sample.

- A second-year resident in psychiatry has been reported to the training director by one of the other residents who has accused him of stalking her. The backstory is that they did go out on a "date" about six weeks earlier but while having dinner in a local restaurant, she became increasingly nervous. He kept making references to sex, intimating that she was in love with him. Her attempts to correct him and change the subject were futile. She told him she had a headache and needed to cut the dinner short and go home. He was upset but did not try to stop her from hailing a taxi and leaving. Since that time, he has been texting her repeatedly. Twice he was waiting at the hospital exit when she was finished for the day. He refuses to stop. The training director met with him and he minimized his actions. The training director also wondered if he might be manic.

- A young neurologist referred herself to CPH. She told the case manager that her work has slipped and her boss is worried about her. She is behind in her charting, her patients have complained that she seems forgetful, and the staff find her dismissive and touchy. She disclosed that she has three young children and she just "kicked her husband out" because "he's abusive" and "doing way too much cocaine." She had psychotherapy during her residency but can't afford it now, and she's stressed.

- A mid-career anesthesiologist called CPH and stated "My boss told me to call you or I'm fired." Asked to elaborate, he's guarded, but did acknowledge that he failed a workplace administered urine screening test for Fentanyl. He admits to diverting drugs "once only" but "they don't believe me." Since being in a motorcycle accident two years ago, he's had a lot of pain. He's under the care of a pain specialist "but that's not working."

- A middle-aged primary care physician has contacted CPH for advice. He lost his license in another state after failing to work with their physician health program. He was given a diagnosis of "polysubstance abuse," namely marijuana, alcohol, benzodiazepines and methamphetamine. Twice he signed abstinence contracts but did not cooperate with monitoring. He was reported to the licensing board and given another chance to get help. He refused and kept practicing medicine, so his license was revoked. This was seven years ago. He was diagnosed with bipolar illness six years ago and has been "clean and sober" since. He's been working as a realtor, and would now like to take refresher courses and, hopefully, win back his license to practice medicine again.

My many years as a doctors' doctor in private practice have served me well in being of assistance to the physicians referred to CPH. This work is different than private practice. When I meet the physician, it is once only, and with no expectation of continuing care. "Independent" means being at arm's length from the physician and anyone involved in their training, employment or treatment. There can be no conflict of interest. That visit is usually three hours long, and entails gathering information both current and historical, as well as collateral information - with the doctors' signed consent - from employers or training directors, anyone who is treating the person currently or in the recent past, and one or more significant others, like family, medical colleagues, or close friends. I also obtain and review old records of treatment, and then submit the lengthy completed report to CPH. My goal is for my evaluations to be fair, accurate, clear, and helpful to everyone, especially the referred physicians.

Medical Student Advocacy

Another way of using my experience in physician health is serving on the College of Medicine Admissions Committee, which I've been doing for a number of years at SUNY Downstate Health Sciences University. I am the only psychiatrist with lengthy clinical experience on the committee, so I'm tasked with interviewing a specific group of applicants, the ones who openly write that they have suffered from mental health symptoms in the past. This is a sea change in medical education, refreshing and long overdue. Most applicants to medical school do not, nor are they required to, reveal that information. Competition is fierce for a spot in each year's matriculating classes across the nation, and compounding that is how much the entire process is mired in stigma. And not just stigma attached to psychiatric illness.

Applicants are reluctant, if not terrified, to disclose anything about themselves that they fear could signify them as inferior, unworthy, or other. That they would be denied entrance into the "hallowed halls" (quotation marks are intentional, as is a bit of sarcasm) of medical education.

And that is why I look forward to interviewing these courageous young women and men. I review their applications the day before so that I'm well prepared to ask not only the standard questions about their interest in medicine, their GPA and MCAT scores, study habits, volunteerism, research and stress-relieving activities, but also their disclosure. I've created below a composite and disguised example of what I might read embedded in the Personal Comments section of an application.

In my final year of high school, my parents separated. I was okay at first because I could see it coming, and I was relieved. I couldn't wait to get away to college. But their divorce was ugly and they both leaned on me. During my second semester, my grades fell badly. But I studied harder and pulled them up, sort of. Then in my sophomore year, I couldn't focus and got down. It took me a long time to go to student health counseling. But I did. That helped, and so did pills for depression. I still take them. But this explains why I made the Dean's List only in my junior and senior years. There's a lot of depression in my family. And my dad's dad killed himself before I was born.

I am careful and respectful when I interview a candidate with this kind of story. Despite what they've written in their essay, they may not wish to elaborate. Asking blanket questions about medical and psychiatric conditions, including substance use disorders, is illegal, but interviewers are permitted to ask applicants about their ability to perform the functions of a medical student and whether they may require reasonable accommodations. Hence, with the above scenario as an example, and his mentioning still taking pills, I might ask the applicant if he's currently in care. And if so, are his medications being monitored by a psychiatrist or primary care physician. I would like to have a sense of how he's currently doing and whether he feels back to his baseline, and if he believes he's ready to tackle the academic expectations of medical school. I would also apprise him of the counseling service at our school that is available to medical students. I am mindful of the context, that I'm interviewing a candidate for medical school, not a new patient in my office. The rules of privilege and access are profoundly different.

I ask a question like this: "Your decision to be transparent about your mental health history in your application is commendable. Tell me about that?" Most say that this was a decision that took significant time. They have usually shared their inclination to be open with their parents, partner or spouse, pre-health commit-tee advisor, or therapist – and may have received mixed advice. But mostly they say things like this: "At the end of the day, I felt strongly that I needed to include this, to be authentic. This is a part of who I am. I know what it's like to be ill, vulnerable, and to seek professional help. My doctors have been wonderful. And inspirational. Having been a patient myself, I can better empa-thize with my patients. I also know what I found so helpful in a doctor and what I didn't. I think that this journey will make me a better doctor." Can't argue with that! And after a brief pause, most add this sentence: "And if a medical school that I've applied to doesn't like what I've written and tosses my application in the waste basket, then I don't want to study medicine there."

After interviewing candidates like this, I invariably reflect on how far we've come in medicine from when I applied to school back in the 1960s. It gives me great pleasure to know that these highly talented young doctors of tomorrow refuse to be hamstrung or deterred by their humanness, their vulnerabilities. That they have the resolve to challenge the archaic and dangerous confines of stigma that affect so many of today's physicians. To put an end to the needless suffering.

In the words of Nelson Mandela: *"The youth of today are the leaders of tomorrow."*

References

1. Michael F. Myers, *Why Physicians Die by Suicide: Lessons Learned from Their Families and Others Who Cared* (New York: Michael F Myers/Amazon Publishing, 2017) 23-24.

2. E.A. Baxter "Personal accounts: Turn of the tide," *Psychiatric Services Journal* 49 (October 1,1998) 1297-98. https://doi.org/10.1176/ps.49.10.1297.

3. Michael F. Myers, "Pearls of Wisdom From Four Women Who Have Lost a Physician Loved One to Suicide," *Psychiatry and Behavioral Health Learning Network* (June 20, 2018) https://www.psychcongress.com/blog/pearls-wisdom-four-women-who-have-lost-physician-loved-one-suicide.

4. Mark Vonnegut, *The Eden Express: A Memoir of Insanity* (New York: Seven Stories Press, 1975)

5. Francis K. Conley MD, *Walking Out on the Boys* (New York: Farrar, Straus and Giroux, 1999)

6. Sherwin B. Nuland, *How We Die: Reflections on Life's Final Chapter* (New York: Vintage Books/Alfred A Knopf, 1993)

7. Carla Fine, *No Time to Say Goodbye: Surviving the Suicide of a Loved One* (New York: Harmony Books/ Penguin Random House, 1999)

8. http://www.mssny.org/cph/

Chapter Ten

Reflections on What My Doctor-Patients Have Taught Me

"Medicine is learned by the bedside and not in the classroom. Let not your conceptions of disease come from the words heard in the lecture room or read from the book."

Charles S. Bryan, *Osler: Inspirations from a Great Physician* (New York: Oxford University Press, 1997) 114.

P hysicians, myself included, at the end of a lecture or in the acknowledgments section of a scientific paper or book, commonly thank their patients. Two examples are: "My patients have been my best teachers. They've taught me everything I know about medicine" and the corollary: "I thank them for entrusting me with their care." When I think about Sir William Osler's quote above, how it rings true! When I first started seeing physician patients back in the early 1970s, there was no classroom

I could attend or book I could read to learn about how to treat doctors. The sources of my learning were at the bedside of my hospitalized doctor-patients and in my private office, and here is what my experiences have taught me.

To always strive for excellence

The pursuit of excellence is the cornerstone of medical education and its practitioners. What physician would not ascribe to this unadorned tenet? To always try to make the right diagnosis and plan the correct treatment. This is simply good medicine and ethically sound. And medico-legally wise.

Because I treat doctors, I have felt that there's another dimension to my quest to excel, that the bar is set a little higher. My patients, being physicians themselves, come with a set of expectations that not all lay patients bring. They have trained in medicine, and even though they've studied a different specialty than me - except of course my psychiatrist patients - they can sense and observe my adherence to professional standards, behaviors, appearance and language. I started out long before individuals routinely went through an Internet search before seeing a new doctor, but the majority have done some type of research before consulting me. This might have been by word of mouth, by talking to a doctor colleague who found seeing me helpful, by meeting me in person in the doctors' lounge, or by attending a lecture I'd given or reading an article that I'd published. This process is common when physicians go to psychiatrists and is fundamentally about personal fit. Is this the kind of doctor who seems easy to talk to and who listens? Who's smart but not arrogant? Who's clear and practical without being precipitous? Who's interested in my story and not just prescribing medication?

There is yet another piece to this. When a doctor becomes my patient, I expect that they will project onto me a level of care they expect of themselves. If I don't meet that standard, then my patient is going to be confused, upset and disappointed. I try of course to watch for this so we can discuss it. If I think this is an impossible benchmark for me, I say so. If I've fallen short, and I too can understand my patient's frustration, then I apologize and agree to do better.

Dr. Fox, a urologist, came to see me on the advice of his brother, an endocrinologist who was also my patient. He started with: "I'm really lost, not sure what to do with myself, I hate going home after work. I get restless and bored." He told me that he had left his wife about eighteen months earlier for another woman. But that didn't work out. He was now living on his own and hated it. We began to meet weekly for psychotherapy. But after four visits, he came in with this: "This isn't working. I'm ready to say 'adios.' I'm no better than I was before I met you. You got my brother on an antidepressant and he's more like himself again. Can't you do the same for me? I'm depressed, too." I tried to explain that his mood change was situational and that we needed to focus on his new life, becoming more comfortable with himself, looking at his self-esteem and his dependency on others, and his choices in women. He didn't disagree but countered with: "But this is taking too long, shouldn't I know myself better by now." I replied: "Four weeks is not a long time. I wonder if you're using a surgical lens here. That if we could just get out a scalpel and cut out the diseased part, then you could be on your way." He laughed, sort of, and added: "Well, I do love the surgical part of my work. Especially big cases. I love the challenge, and the adventure. And making my patients happy. It all happens pretty fast." I replied: "I think we've got a lot in common as physicians. Where we differ is that my work isn't procedural, it takes longer." From then on Dr. Fox was much calmer and more forbearing. And he made great progress over the next few months.

What I feel inside is that I'm being observed, scrutinized, and at times judged by my doctor-patients. And why not, because when you put yourself out there as a subspecialist, are you not opening yourself up to examination and review? And that's the reason why I not only endorse lifelong learning and continuing medical education, but practice it dutifully. In my teaching of psychiatric residents and early-career psychiatrists about treating medical students and physicians, I drive home this point. Recently, one of my students made this very poignant statement: "My grandmother used to say that getting older wasn't for 'sissies.' I think that looking after our own isn't for 'sissies,' either."

Her remark reminded me of a statement that one of my psychiatrist colleagues made to me several years ago: "I don't know how you do it Mike, looking after all of us docs. Not for me. I wouldn't be able to get away with my usual bullshit. They'd see right through me." I laughed because I get him. He's a superb psychiatrist, and his patients, all with chronic mental illness and mostly in shelters or living on the streets, love him. He can hunker down. Even the most paranoid trust him as best they can.

Humility

> *"I have never entirely escaped the view that being a doctor is something of a moral luxury, by which doctors are easily corrupted. We can so easily end up complacent and self-important, feeling ourselves to be more important than our patients."*

Henry Marsh, *Life as a Brain Surgeon* (New York: Picador/Macmillan, 2018) 31.

My doctor-patients have taught me humility. Many of them are complex, and they've challenged my competency and skills. Some have fired me. Some have threatened to sue or report me to the medical licensing board. Some have taken their lives. With this comes infinite soul searching, and a degree of professional modesty, an acceptance of my limitations. It's become easier to say: "I don't know." And to see my mistakes, to sit with them, and to apologize. Psychiatrist Dr. Aaron Lazare put it crisply: "One of the most profound human interactions is the offering and accepting of apologies."[1]

I do not believe that these realizations or insights into myself are unique to those who treat physicians. They are the trajectory of all clinicians as the years of practice lengthen. No way of proving it, but I would argue that treating physicians has hastened or enhanced a particular kind of humbleness in me. And this has served me well, not just for personal gain, but for my professional growth. I will explain in a minute, but first, a paradox. One of the common pitfalls in becoming a subspecialist or expert in anything is egoism. Translation: "I'm a doctors' doctor, highly educated and accomplished individuals come to me for treatment. Some are luminaries in their field. They trust and respect me. I must be more than good." But acclaim does not always equate with results. And one can possess a healthy level of self-confidence and still remain humble.

How does humility manifest itself in the doctor-patient relationship? I've written in detail about this elsewhere[2] but here's a summary:

- Accept that a healthy and mutually respectful relationship is essential. The foundation of good care.

- Respond quickly when a physician calls for an appointment. These are not easy calls for a symptomatic doctor to make, so a prompt, welcoming and interested response is paramount.

- Make that first visit comprehensive, yet invite the patient to speak openly and freely, and without too much interruption. Convey a diagnosis or differential diagnosis that may be tentative, yet clear and in lay language. Ditto for a treatment plan or therapeutic approach. And save time to ask for questions.

- Always use an empathic approach.

- Be open to a second opinion, especially when treatment is not progressing within the parameters of usual care.

- Keep an interest in interviewing loved ones, both to learn more and to answer questions, assuage fears, and at times enlist their help.

Many of my doctor-patients have mirrored humility in my office, and I have tried hard to capture and emulate their posture. How can you not when you are present at their diminishment, vulnerability, simple humanness, and rawness in their hour of need? Many have been brought to their knees by their battles with alcohol or depression, ugly divorces, dismissal from their jobs, or suspension of their medical license. As they make progress, begin to feel better, understand themselves in more depth and reach a healthy stage of pondering and expansive thinking, some utter statements like this: "I think there's a silver lining to this nightmare. It's changed me. I'm a nicer person. Kinder." I've been tempted to blurt out "me too," but I don't.

Here's an example:

Dr. Norris, a radiologist, came to see me in the throes of leaving her husband, a transplant surgeon. Her children were now on their own and she finally felt emancipated, free to extract herself from a stifling, abusive marriage. She did well for the first six months or so, but she developed a recurrence of a depression that she experienced years earlier after the birth of her second child. She fell fast, nearly attempted suicide, and I had to hospitalize her. But she prevailed, responded nicely to treatment, and was safe to leave after three weeks. I looked after her for about five years.

I want to highlight here what kind of a person she was. Highly accomplished, Dr. Norris headed her department, one of the few women chairs at that time. This came with an international reputation in her field, and accolades and national awards outside of medicine for her pioneering role modeling for women's achievement. We worked at the same medical center, where she was a household name. When I needed to hospitalize her, I planned to have a colleague look after her at another hospital, respecting her privacy. She would have none of it. She insisted on being treated where we both worked. She allayed any awkwardness in the nursing staff, or anxiety in the medical students or residents, by just being her authentic self. She never pulled rank, and all of the trainees involved in her care marveled at her disposition. She was warm and expressive and full of gratitude for all we did for her.

Dr. Norris's humility was a gift to me, and one that extended beyond myself. Just after I signed her release and she left the ward to go home, both the medical student and psychiatry resident who assisted me in her care talked about the impression she made on them. They admired what kind of patient she had been— very ill, but not embarrassed to be a doctor-patient on a mental health service. How she bore her illness with fortitude, dignity, and grace. How kind she was toward them. And should they ever be admitted to a psychiatric unit themselves, that remembering her might make the experience of it less burdensome for them.

Complexity of Physicians

Decades of assessing and treating physicians has taught me a basic lesson, that they can be complicated, tough to diagnose, and hard to treat. What makes them complex seems to be a tension, a dynamic interplay between their personality makeup, their medical knowledge and the culture of medicine. Let me break this down.

Physicians come in all shapes and sizes. I'm being careful not to simplify or reduce their personalities to stereotypes, but there are traits that stand out. One of these is perfectionism. Should a physician develop psychiatric symptoms, like anxiety, self-doubts, low spirits, or obsessional thinking, these may be very hard for them to accept. The physician begins to self-diagnose. Instead of feeling proud that she's made the correct diagnosis, she feels the opposite, scared and embarrassed. Instead of accepting that she's developing hallmarks of an illness, she feels flawed, which is hard when you're usually super-competent and confident. Strike one. Even if the doctor "confesses" these changes to family members or close friends, they may be baffled and not always be supportive because they're so accustomed to her being on top of her game. Strike two. How accepting or understanding is the world of medicine, predicated as it is on selective competition, exclusivity, excellence and pride? Strike three.

Added to this mix is a paradoxical tendency for doctors to delay going for help. One would think that faced with symptoms a physician would dash off to their doctor. Not so in this case. When doctors wait a long time before seeking help, their condition might worsen and become harder to treat. Or they might get into trouble at work because their symptoms affect their behavior - they're late for clinic, become testy and irritable, or grow flat and detached. Some might start treating themselves with drug samples or self-prescribing, which they often don't get right, thereby developing side-effects like drowsiness or loss of technical coordination. Too many drown their troubles in alcohol, which only worsens the original condition, and provokes the added risk of developing the co-morbidity of a substance use disorder.

This is what I mean by complexity. At the point that they become a patient these individuals may already be quite ill, and this needs to be recognized and accepted by the treating psychiatrist. Judging the doctor for so many self-defeating behaviors is unacceptable and unprofessional. I have found it best to simply accept the old adage "It is what it is." And I try my best to be patient and understanding with such difficult and interwoven issues, in that for physicians becoming a patient is a process not an event. Many rookie psychiatrists get impatient with doctor-patients and expect a different response from them because they're physicians. "She should know better" is the refrain. I tell them it's best to forget that she's a doctor, and that once you get to know her, you'll find that there are all kinds of personal and family reasons that explain her actions.

A final word about complexity. My most problematic physician patients have required more than my care. In fact, I've learned the hard way on this one, that it's been too much to bear for me to manage them on my own. That I do a better job, and my patient gets better treatment, if the responsibility is shared with other health professionals, such as a psychologist, primary care physician, psychopharmacologist, addiction medicine specialist, forensic professional, clergy person, or physician coach. When I gave a talk on my treatment of Dr. Z, described in Chapter Seven above, my acknowledgement slide listed twelve physicians, a clinical social worker, and a host of psychiatric nurses who assisted me in his care.

Professional Confidence

I am indebted to my doctor patients for this. I've probably gained the most from the ones who have frustrated me, the ones who pushed my buttons, who have seemed dismissive or antagonistic toward my efforts. They've forced me to look inward, to examine my role in their behaviors, to search for a calmer response to them. The gift of equanimity. This has resulted in my being less intimidated by the battle-worn patients, the ones who have seen many previous mental health professionals, and who come with a negative or skeptical attitude, not hopeful that anyone can help. Having a healthy degree of professional confidence enables me to be of aid, even if that means simply acknowledging what they're living with, their years of suffering, or misfortune. And that I've acquired the wisdom to recognize when I need to refer them to a colleague near or far with special expertise. This can restore a bit of hope in forlorn people.

Courage

Looking after so many physicians has given me tenacity. And audacity. This has fueled my efforts at advocacy, a much-needed effort on behalf of physicians. At times, I've been appalled at how shabbily my physician patients have been treated by their training directors, heads of academic departments, hospital employers, medical licensing boards, clinic partners, and disability insurers. Writing strong letters on their behalf has been one form my campaign has taken in this arena. Speaking out, composing reports, and fighting for change in my governance committee work are others. When psychiatrically ill doctors are mistreated because of ignorance, my goal is educating. When it's meanness or discrimination, my objective is to work with my patient together with their legal counsel.

In my teaching of junior colleagues about treating physicians, I consistently highlight advocacy. Too many psychiatrists – and other mental health professionals – are limited in their sights. They restrict their work to what they do behind closed doors, the specifics of the treatment process. They do not accept that their responsibility to their patient often extends beyond that enterprise. That they have an essential role to play in fighting workplace, insurance, or licensure injustices – and how these factors block their patients' improvement and wellbeing. Psychiatry stands out in the world of medicine as the most stigmatized specialty, and stigma has to be fought with heart and soul. And sometimes you have to call in the big guns.

As I mentioned earlier, when I wrote about certain of my patients mirroring humility, I've had other patients and medical acquaintances display courage and gallantry that I've learned from. You can't help but want to emulate them, or learn from them, or borrow from them to use in your teaching of others. Here are two notable examples.

First, this passage by psychiatrist Dr. Linda Gask, who has written about her long struggle with depression: "I've spent most of my life helping people to patch up their souls in order to keep going and accepting help from others in repairing my own... Unfortunately, many societies, including our own, are not ready for such a level of honesty, but I know that my depression is not something I should be – or am – ashamed of."[3]

Second, while attending a conference in London a couple of years ago, I watched a live and very moving interview with Dr. Robin Warshafsky, lead general practitioner of a healthcare NHS trust. He was talking about losing his son Julien, who was training in anesthesiology, to an overdose of Fentanyl in 2016.[4] In the midst of the conversation he admitted to having suffered from a mood disorder in the past. When asked about speaking so openly about this, he replied: "I wear my depression on my sleeve – no one is going to make me feel ashamed." I loved what he said and I've used this quote in a number of my lectures since. There's a defiant quality to his words, a defiance that is so refreshing, overdue, and necessary.

Gratitude

Face to face with dying, neurologist Dr. Oliver Sacks, reflecting upon his life, expressed gratitude with an eloquence and fluidity of pen that is stunning.[5] I cannot count the number of times I've reread his essay. One sentence in particular stands out for me: "I have had an intercourse with the world, the special intercourse of writers and readers." Writing here, my circumstances are different than those of Oliver Sacks at that time, but my strong feelings of gratitude are the same. And therefore, I shall add a word of my own to his second phrase, so that now it reads "... the special intercourse of writers and readers *and psychiatrists*."

A cardiac surgeon patient of mine, I'll call him Dr. Gore, now recovered from a devastating and crippling depression, was saying goodbye in his final visit. Here's the dialogue:

"Dr. Gore: Thank you for saving my life.

Me: Thank you for that. You must get compliments like that often in your work.

Dr. Gore: Yes, but this is different.

Me: How so?

Dr. Gore: I get my patients breathing better, less chest pain, walking better, functioning better. Sometimes they get back to work. They get more time.

Me: That's a lot, no?

Dr. Gore: But, this is different. You gave me my life back. I can think again. I can remember things. I can read and learn new things now. I can operate. And I can feel emotions. I can appreciate opera again. I got the love for my wife back, and the kids, and my grandkids. You've given me hope, another kick at the can. It doesn't get much better than that."

Though I'm not sure I totally agree with Dr. Gore, that's beside the point, because there are many ways of saving a life. And how do you measure gratitude? But I was grateful for the chance to help Dr. Gore. He was in the midst of a severe major depressive episode when we met, a shell of the man adored by his family and beloved by his patients and students. He required a four-week hospital stay, followed by a partial hospitalization program, a fancy cocktail of medication, and intensive cognitive behavior therapy, but it all came together nicely over about six months. Gratitude goes out to the whole team of expert professionals, to his loving attentive family, and to his colleagues at work who kept in touch with emails, text messages, cards, and personal visits.

I grew up in a home that practiced the professional courtesy of looking after one's own when they were in need. My attorney father extended this to other lawyers in town, including law students, whenever they needed legal advice or assistance. When I was a medical student, many of my professors and attending physicians looked after each other and their families. When I opened my private practice in 1973, universal healthcare was already in place in Canada, meaning that practicing professional courtesy no longer included a monetary or financial break to your physician patient. Physicians bill the medical plan, not the patient, and are paid in full. I've been conditioned to help my brothers and sisters in medicine; hence, the evolution of my restricted practice and focus on doctors and their families.

There is an interesting, and rather humorous, back story here. When I initiated my specialized practice, my secretary was the first contact person, the one whom people spoke to. If a doctor's office called to refer a patient, or if the patient called directly, she'd ask if the person was a physician. Most weren't, so she'd respond with this: "I'm terribly sorry but Dr. Myers has a limited practice, he only sees doctors and their families." Not uncommonly, the caller would reply with something like this: "What? He can't do that. That's not fair. I'm a taxpayer. That's elitist." Ever the mature professional that she was, she'd respond calmly with this: "Again, I'm sorry. But let me explain. Dr. Myers believes that by looking after physicians, by keeping them well, they are better able to practice excellent medicine and provide good care to all of their patients." Whereupon the caller, now lost for words, would say: "Oh my god, I never knew that doctors could have troubles or get sick. That makes sense, what he's doing. Tell him to keep up his important work."

This is another dimension to my gratitude— that I was able to practice psychiatry in a system that worked both for my patients and for me. They didn't have to worry whether I accepted their insurance or not – or whether they could afford me if I didn't take insurance. If I turned away a new or potential doctor patient, it was never about ability to pay, rather it was due to my inability to accommodate a new patient based on my workload and schedule.

Acceptance of Loss

"When I was a kid, there was this sadness to her... that has permeated her life. As a young kid, I didn't know the origins of it... that loss, she never talked about it... So the very idea of survival became interesting to me...why certain people survive and others don't. So, serving in war zones...I understood the language of loss...it's not that I'm stopping it...or doing anything about it...but I do think there is

something about bearing witness…and asking other people to bear witness to it as well…"

Anderson Cooper, *Nothing Left Unsaid: Gloria Vanderbilt & Anderson Cooper* (New York: HBO/ HD, 2016) 190 min.

My doctor-patients have given me an encyclopedic knowledge of loss, its types, and its ramifications. And this has been more than an intellectual understanding of loss, for it has included a process of appreciating the panoply of emotions that accompany loss. Many of these feelings are uncomfortable for any therapist working with grieving patients, and it takes time and seasoning to be able to be present and effective with such patients. This is a gift from my patients, a strength that I've acquired through treating them while they are in the midst of and healing from their losses.

In an earlier chapter in this book, I focused on AIDS in the early years. All of my HIV-positive medical students and physicians, including those who had developed AIDS, were dealing with various losses or anticipated losses. Examples were losing one's body integrity and strength, coming to terms with the discoloration of one's skin and disfigurement by Kaposi's sarcoma, the assault to one's attractiveness because of losing fat on one's face and limbs or developing a thick neck or buffalo hump. Other losses included one's privacy about being gay or bisexual, because the disease and its treatment pushes many out of the closet. Another loss is occupational, not being able to practice procedural medicine because of risk of contaminating one's patients with the virus. An anticipated loss of a shortened life and, until the mid-1990s, an inevitable death sentence. Having to abandon dreams of finding a partner, or sustaining an intimate relationship, starting a family, growing old together. Or being HIV positive and losing one's life partner to AIDS. All examples of other losses.

In another chapter I focused on my decades of being a marital therapist for doctors. In this work, my patients taught me about other kinds of losses. Most couples in the throes of marital unhappiness and tension are grieving: the loss of a working partnership, the loss of mutual happiness, the loss of personal happiness, the loss of the ability to talk with each other, the loss of a co-parenting allegiance, the loss of self-esteem when there's abuse, the loss of sexual intimacy, the loss of financial security in the face of professional failure, or finally the loss of a solid, secure future together. While treating couples and individual doctors trying to navigate through a divorce, new losses arose: loss of one's home, loss of daily access to one's children, loss of financial security, loss of sameness and predictability, loss of one's neighborhood and supports, loss of extended family on the spouse's side.

My doctor-patients experiencing major psychiatric illness have taught me about a whole other series of losses. Some of these have been in training when they had their first bout of depression or mania and the diagnosis of bipolar illness was made. And even if they've responded well to treatment and have a good prognosis, they recognize that their dream of being a pediatric neurosurgeon may need reconsideration. That the reality of several demanding postgraduate years of training, including very long days, operating in the middle of the night, and limited personal and family time, is not compatible with what is required to live well with a mood disorder. Most choose another specialty better suited to these realities, but it is, at least at first, a loss for them. Other of my physician patients have been forced to accept that recovery from their depression, post-traumatic stress disorder, or obsessive-compulsive disorder has not been 100 percent. They have to live with residual symptoms, like less energy, the attrition of their ability to multitask or their capacity to feel a normal range of emotions. This means that they can't return to work full time or must abandon aspects of their work that they can no longer comfortably do. Again, another type of loss. Here's an example:

Dr. Fuller, an early mid-career psychiatrist, worked three days a week on the forensic unit of a psychiatric hospital with severely ill psychotic patients. Trained in psychoanalytic psychotherapy, she looked after higher functioning patients the other two days in her private practice. She was happy with her life. Unfortunately, in her mid-40s, a depressive illness that first hit her in medical school (but responded nicely to antidepressants and counseling) returned with a vengeance. Despite my best efforts, and those of a psychopharmacologist, Dr. Fuller never completely got better. She could do her hospital work but not her private practice. She put it like this: "I use a different skill set there. I'm a physician using everything I learned in medical school about doctoring, overseeing my patients' physical health, ordering lab work, monitoring their psychiatric medications, giving ECT, working with my team, counseling their families. My psychoanalytic work with my private patients is so different. I no longer have the focus, the ability to listen carefully, resonate with their feelings and words, go to dark and frightening places with them. And I've lost my creativity. I have to give this up, it's not fair to them, and it's not safe. It makes me sad to do this but I know I have to. I'm in mourning for what I've loved so much for so many years."

Throughout my years of treating doctors dealing with so much loss, I became aware of a shift in the tone and quality of the doctor-patient relationship, but it was confusing, elusive and unclear to me. Until a moment of serendipity. I was in the library of the Royal Society of Medicine in London poring over archives about the history of doctor suicide in the United Kingdom. Suddenly, I came upon a document, the likes of which I had never encountered before. It was called "Report of an Independent Inquiry into the Care and Treatment of Daksha Emson M.B.B.S., MRCPsych, MSc. and Her Daughter Freya."[6] I was mesmerized with its contents and spent much of my time on the flight home to New York the next morning carefully examining its sixty-plus pages. Over the next couple of days, I tried to find an email for David Emson, Dr. Emson's surviving husband, but to no avail. But I found an address and wrote him a letter, and to my delight he received it and contacted me. Thus began our relationship, and although neither David nor his wife were my patients, I am indebted to him (and the memory of Daksha) for helping me understand and name that "something" I've alluded to above. It's a feeling of closeness, of warmth. Let me illustrate with portions of a blog piece that I wrote about two years later titled "The Intimacy of Tragedy."[7]

"As I alight from the Tube in London's East End I see the man I've come to visit. We've never met in person but we hug with affection like old friends.

Our two-year relationship consists of intermittent email correspondence and a telephone call over a year ago. We turn from the station and head toward his home. Normally a fifteen-minute walk, we take an hour, conversing non-stop and pausing frequently to minimize distractions. We stop by the school where his wife completed her primary education. I am listening more than talking – and that is exactly what I want. I am thinking to myself about the power of tragedy and how its horror builds intimacy between people. I feel like I've known this man all my life."

Dave is a freshwater palaeoecologist and retired specialist radiographer. He lost his wife Daksha, a psychiatrist, and their 3-month-old daughter Freya to "extended suicide" almost seventeen years ago, in October of 2000.

"Daksha came to the UK from India with her family at the age of 8, speaking little English. A gifted student, she easily won acceptance to the Royal London Hospital Medical College. She was diagnosed with depression after a serious suicide attempt in medical school. Initial treatment worked but her recovery was short-lived, as she had a number of relapses requiring many different medications, hospitalizations and courses of ECT. After a manic episode, she was diagnosed with bipolar illness. Her medical studies took longer than usual but, as her husband stated, 'she distinguished herself by obtaining first-place in all her exams, coming second in the whole of the University of London, despite missing most of her lectures due to hospitalizations and sitting her exams in the aftermath of depression' and she won a large number of academic awards. She completed residency training in psychiatry and received her MRCPsych certificate as well as a MSc in mental health studies. Her research interests were in both forensic and community psychiatry.

"Dave and Daksha were married for eight years and he told me that she never experienced a relapse during that time. She came off her medication while trying to become pregnant and experienced three consecutive miscarriages before their longed-for daughter Freya was born on July 4, 2000. She remained off her meds while breast-feeding with the goal of weaning and restarting her Lithium and antidepressant when Freya was 3 months old. However, just a day or two before an appointment with her psychiatrist, she crashed into a delusional psychosis, which she managed to successfully hide from both him and her husband. She hinted at 'evil forces' to her husband as he left for work in the morning. Eight hours later, he returned to a goodbye note on the kitchen table and a house of horrors - the lifeless body of his daughter and his badly burned wife. Daksha had stabbed Freya to death then set them both afire. She died three weeks later in a burn unit."

Dave and I spent four hours together, talking in his kitchen over more than one cup of tea. He was approaching the 17th anniversary of losing Daksha and Freya. Passage of time has eased his pain a little bit. He told me about his PTSD and how treatment has helped him. He's wistful. Humble. Grateful for his environmental work, grateful for the love of his neighbors.

"With the afternoon waning and much time passing, I mention that I need to be running along. As we leave to walk back to the station, Dave asks me if he can give me a gift. I am jarred by his humility (he is asking me for permission to give a gift, not a pronouncement that he'd like to give me a gift). I blurt out: 'Of course!' It is a framed photo of a beaming Daksha and Freya taken by Dave in their garden two days before their deaths. I am speechless. My misty, rapidly blinking eyes are not lost on

him. Dave adds that he lost both of his parents over the past two years and this photo was theirs, a gift from him after the funeral.

"Our walk back to the train takes only fifteen minutes this time. We hug again, wave goodbye and away I go, not before turning back and waving again. I bound on to the crowded train and take a deep breath. And another. And one more."

References

1. Aaron Lazare, *On Apology* (New York: Oxford University Press, 2004) 1.

2. Michael F. Myers, *Why Physicians Die by Suicide: Lessons Learned from Their Families and Others Who Cared* (New York: Michael F. Myers/Amazon Publishing, 2017) 111-19.

3. Linda Gask, *The Other Side of Silence: A Psychiatrist's Memoir of Depression*. (West Sussex UK: Vie Books/Summerside Publishers Ltd, 2015) 257.

4. Clare Dyer, "Julien Warshafsky: How this doctor died and what it tells about the system that failed him," *British Medical Journal* 361(k2564) doi:10:1093 (June 14, 2018)

5. Oliver Sacks, "My Own Life." *New York Times* Editorial. February 19, 2015. https://www.nytimes.com/2015/02/19/opinion/oliver-sacks-on-learning-he-has-terminal-cancer.html

6. http://www.simplypsychiatry.co.uk/sitebuildercontent/sitebuilderfiles/deinquiryreport.pdf

7. Michael F. Myers, "The Intimacy of Tragedy," October 7, 2016. https://www.psychcongress.com/blog/intimacy-tragedy.

Conclusion:
The Future is Bright

May 21, 2020. I started today by attending a virtual funeral for a colleague of mine, a psychiatrist, who died of Covid-19 on May 4, 2020. Dr. Andrew "Drew" Slaby was 77 years old. All churches being closed because of the pandemic, the service began with a blessing outside of St. Teresa of Avila in Summit, New Jersey. Drew's companion, Rosemarie Dackerman, spoke a few words outside. An hour later, the service resumed with interment of his ashes at Christ Church Memorial Garden in Short Hills, New Jersey.

The minister said a few words, as did Rosemarie. She invited anyone attending by Zoom to speak. And many mourners did, including myself. Several voiced their frustration and sorrow at not being able to be physically present to hug her, and Drew's family and close friends, yet their sweet memories of Drew as a kind and caring man and physician eclipsed the physical distance imposed by the virus. It was remarkably intimate. Rosemarie announced that she would hold a celebration of Drew's life in the fall, when hopefully the "new normal" will permit an in-person gathering. The service concluded with her placing individual mauve roses near the urn.

I have opened my concluding chapter with this story because, despite its sadness, the future **is** bright. Drew was a man who modeled that kind of light. A brilliant clinician and lauded educator, he had boundless energy, social facility, and an infectious smile. He was a prolific author with a large breadth of focus. Our clinical experiences overlapped, especially in suicidology. He was supportive of my efforts in the field of physician health and I thank him for that. His was a life well lived.

At noon on May 21, 2020, I attended a virtual town hall meeting of the College of Medicine faculty hosted by our Dean, Dr. Charles Brunicardi. There were reports from various committees, as usual, but it was a relief to hear, confirmed by data, that the apex of Covid-19 seemed to be behind us, as we now enter the recovery phase. Monday April 6, 2020 will be etched forever in my memory, the day that our hospital University Hospital Brooklyn had the highest number of deaths of Covid-19 patients - seventeen. Two days later, April 8th, at our weekly support meeting for hospitalists, I remember the doctors talking about the volume of severely ill patients, many on respirators, many on oxygen awaiting respirators. They were working so hard and fighting a sense of futility, in the face of such suffering, and in the isolation of their patients from their families who were not allowed into the hospital.

Toward the end of March 2020, New York Governor Andrew Cuomo designated the 375-bed University Hospital of Brooklyn, where I work, a COVID-19-only facility. Anticipating a surge of critically-ill patients for our frontline staff, psychiatrist colleague Dr. Ramaswamy Viswanathan and I began offering weekly virtual support groups - one for hospitalist physicians, and another for emergency medicine physicians. In the early weeks, physicians spoke openly as they described their anxiety about contracting the virus, about getting sick themselves and possibly dying, about transmitting the virus to their families at home, and about inadvertently infecting each other should their personal protective equipment fail. They admitted to feeling terrified, numb, and surreal, and talked about being demoralized and depressed. Everyone, however, was committed to their work: "This is my calling. This is what I'm trained to do."

Social distancing is the order of the day, but not psychologically. Nobody seems shy or embarrassed about their vulnerability, their humanness.

As I wrote above, coping with the number of dying patients on every shift has been hard for the doctors.[1] They are grieving. This is expressed with emotional and unrestrained language. There is little of the medical jargon or intellectualizing so common and historical in medical settings. Here are several quotes: "My heart aches, my chest is so heavy and it gets heavier as the day goes on. I can't wait to get all my equipment off and just weep." Another doctor said: "The last two days I think I've lost a pound, all tears, just crying, so sad for people who were my patients for such a short time. And their families." And another: "We all talk about how much we need a hug, but of course we can't hold each other. But there's relief in just saying it, or joking about air hugs."

The barriers of seniority and rank seem to have disappeared in our groups. Attending physicians and residents talk about feelings like peers. They speak from their hearts and guts. One session, on the heels of the tragic loss of a beloved critical care specialist to the virus,[2] was replete with memories, warm anecdotes, and teary testimonials. Losing one of their own makes this nightmare even more terrifying - casualties aren't just strangers; it also happens to us and those we love.

In the concluding chapter of my book *Why Physicians Die by Suicide: Lessons Learned from Their Families and Others Who Cared*, I wrote this:[3]

"If anything, I feel more communal — that this challenge, saving the lives of physicians, requires building bridges and cooperative work… We must continue to be candid and rigorous — and we must keep talking about a subject that, sadly, is not going away. When that day comes, and it will, we can be quiet."

I feel the same way as I conclude this book more than three years later. Doctors are reaching out to each other in both directions, asking for help and offering their help. More and more physicians are talking about their mental health struggles in significant ways, some in private, others publicly. Psychiatrists and other mental health professionals are extending a hand, offering their services, making the care of colleagues a professional priority. And the ever-evolving world of medicine is changing too, with recognition of, and renewed respect for, its physicians. How my heart swells with relief, gratitude and hope.

References

1. Te-Ping Chen, "Hospitals Brace for Mental-Health Crisis Among Doctors and Nurses," *Wall Street Journal.* May 21, 2020 (Michael F. Myers quoted)

2. Del Valle L. A community mourns a Brooklyn physician who died fighting coronavirus. *CNN.* May 20, 2020. Accessed May 28, 2020.

3. Michael F. Myers, *Why Physicians Die by Suicide: Lessons Learned from Their Families and Others Who Care* (New York: Michael F. Myers/ Amazon Publishing, 2017) 161.

Acknowledgments

This book spans a huge period of my life, over which I have been taught and enriched by countless individuals who contributed to my becoming a doctors' doctor. They number in the hundreds and the list keeps growing. They live near and far. I am grateful for their insights, time spent, colleagueship, mentoring and in many cases, abiding friendship. These relationships have strengthened me and remain a core part of who I am. I wish I could name and thank each one on these pages. They remain in my heart.

My editor Andy Kelly has been enthusiastic about this project since we first discussed it last year. He has been a wonderful partner over the months and quietly does his magic, the stuff that good editors do to give sparkle to the writer's awkward and ofttimes erratic prose.

This book, fittingly, is dedicated to my patients. I thank them for allowing me to be their doctor, but my gratitude does not stop there. I could not have taught others without their help. Masked and composite stories of their lives have enabled and enriched my teaching, in the classroom, in plenary lectures, and my writings. Some have given consent to my medical students and residents to sit in on diagnostic or treatment sessions with them. Some have done the same when I have had trainees from abroad spend time with me to learn about physician health. I am especially grateful to those doctors whose actual stories are depicted in this book, and to the sister of Dr Z, Susan Powell. Their permission is a present to physicians everywhere, rooted in a belief, that there is still too much misunderstanding out there, too much stigma, too much needless suffering. My thanks also to my patients' families who share these sentiments.

My parents and my two older brothers are now deceased but they were unwavering in their support of my becoming a physician, then a psychiatrist. My sister Penny and brother John continue that tradition, quietly, with curiosity and love. My former wife Joice accompanied me on this journey of becoming a doctors' doctor for decades. I have many memories of those years and they mean a lot to me. My daughter Briana and son Zachary have been foundational. They lead fascinating lives, abounding and explorative, and I learn from them. Finally, my husband Charles, always kind and fair, gives me the space to focus on my work and writing. Our easy companionship, and deep affection, enable the rest.

Other Books by Michael F Myers, MD

Why Physicians Die by Suicide: Lessons Learned from Their Families and Others Who Cared

The Physician as Patient: A Clinical Handbook for Mental Health Professionals (with Glen O Gabbard, MD)

Touched by Suicide: Hope and Healing After Loss (with Carla Fine)

The Handbook of Physician Health (with Larry S Goldman, MD and Leah J Dickstein, MD)

Intimate Relationships in Medical School: How to Make Them Work

How's Your Marriage? A Book for Men and Women

Men and Divorce

Doctors' Marriages: A Look at the Problems and Their Solutions

D r. Michael F. Myers is a professor of clinical psychiatry at SUNY Downstate Health Sciences University in Brooklyn, New York. He is the author and coauthor of eight previous books dealing with medical students and physicians. He specializes in physician health, and the majority of his private practice was dedicated to treating physicians and their families.

He has held leadership roles in both the Canadian and American Psychiatric Associations and is a past president of the New York City chapter of the American Foundation for Suicide Prevention. Currently, he serves on the advisory board of the Committee for Physician Health of the Medical Society of the State of New York. A recipient of many national and international awards for his work, Myers lectures around the world. He lives in New York City with his husband Charles Edwards.